NEW YORK
PARTIES

THE ART OF HOSTING

JEAN-MICHEL SAVOCA AND BOYCE BRAWLEY
WITH JUDITH CHOATE

RIZZOLI
NEW YORK

First published in the United States of America in 1989 by
RIZZOLI INTERNATIONAL PUBLICATIONS, INC.
300 Park Avenue South, New York, NY 10010

Library of Congress Cataloging-in-Publication Data

Savoca, Jean-Michel.
    New York parties.

    Includes index.
    1. Entertaining.   2. Cookery, International.
3. Menus.   I. Brawley, Boyce.   II. Choate, Judith.
III. Title.
TX731.S324   1989   642′.4   89-45429
ISBN 0-8478-1123-9

Photographs by Jerry Valente and Michael Gluck
Food styling by Richmond Ellis
Edited by Carol McKeown
Designed by Jeff Batzli

Typeset by Rainsford Type, Danbury, Connecticut
Printed and bound by Toppan Printing, Tokyo, Japan

CREDITS

Additional Photographers

Bradley Ollman for "A Victorian Tea," "A Halloween
    Gathering," and "A Chinese Buffet by the Pool"
Bo Parker for interior, "The Equitable Atrium"
Bruce Wolf for foyer, "Unusual Combinations"

Decor

The American Wing Antiques
    of Bridgehampton
E.T. Cronin Designs
Dean and DeLuca
Glacken and Yavar
Goslee and Co.
The Grand Acquisitor of East Hampton
Kitchen Classics of East Hampton
McNabb and Associates for *Les Misérables*
    and *The Phantom of the Opera*
Party Rental Ltd.
Wedgwood China

Interiors for "Unusual Combinations" designed by Joe
    Lombardo

Flowers

Philip Baloun
Flowers by Aquino
Flowers Unltd.
Goslee and Co.
Madderlake
Michael Strabo

Locations

The America Society
Dezerland
The Equitable Atrium
The Seaport Line

Lighting

Frost Lighting
Robert Stortz

Opera Singers

Abigail and
Michael Mancuso

Tenting

HDO Productions
Stamford Tent

Wedding Cakes

Cile Bellefleur-Burbidge
Sylvia Weinstock

In "A Birthday Party for Mickey Mouse," Mickey Mouse
    and Goofy © The Walt Disney Company.

Use of the two photographs of the opening night party of *Les
Misérables*, appearing on pages 103 and 114 is by permission
of Cameron Mackintosh (Overseas) Limited, the proprietor
of the copyright and trademarked materials contained therein.

C O N T E N T S

A K N O W L E D G E M E N T S

Neither parties nor books are created alone. Our sincerest admiration and thanks:

To: Jerry Valente and Michael Gluck, whose photography captured the essence of New York Parties and romanced our food.

Rick Ellis, the food stylist, whose creative input and skills always came through no matter how difficult the circumstances, along with his able assistant, William Smith.

James Goslee for his style.

Philip Baloun and Dominick Farentino for always enhancing nature.

Party Rental Ltd., for when it comes to tables, you're the tops!

Vicky Bijur, our Literary Agent, whose faith in this project never failed.

Ann Klein and Jane Opper of Rizzoli, whose enthusiasm helped turn a dream into reality.

Dick Mealey for his nimble fingers and meeting the challenges of time.

To: Chef Georgine Cavaiola for her appreciation of the very best, her incomparable palate, and her ability to combine the two.

The New York Parties kitchen staff: Ari Spectorman, Fay Richards-Blake, Nino Castro, Lisa Wasserman, Christopher Sheldon, Linda Castro, and Steve Kolyer for their constant inspiration and talents.

Hillary Wyler, Ann Johnson, and Beth Gordon for keeping the "railroad" running and on schedule.

Carole Lee, Rick Rossi, William B. Bailey, Sarah Wilson, Susan Coniff, and Jean-Paul Richard, whose contributions will long be remembered and always acknowledged.

All the waiters and waitresses, past and present, who have represented New York Parties with skill, smiles, and pride.

—A special thanks to Jacquie Lowry, Tom Nichols, Dan Williams, John Basil, Jerry Thayer, and James Phillips, who direct and teach with grace.

Estelle Green, who believed in us and filled our beginnings with love and encouragement.

Our family members Camille Limardi and Lois and Anthony Tilocca, whose smiles and hard work turned those early years into a joyful family project.

To: Alain Eclache and Jean-Sebastien Szwarc of Les Diables des Lombards, Paris, for fifteen years of fun with food.

Chip Sills, Ellie Karr, and Carole Dixon, whose challenges always put our creativity to the test.

James McIntyre, Anne Thomas, and the Board of Directors of Carnegie Hall, who gave us a home where we learned that a memorable performance comes from dedicated practice.

Helen Tucker and Ruth Feder for teaching us to view any shortcoming as an opportunity for growth.

Chris Giftos and Steve Pagano of The Metropolitan Museum of Art, whose panache has inspired us.

Peter Prestcott and Susan Wyler who always lovingly share and teach.

Courtenay Daniels for being such a great fan and friend.

Robert and Richard Rathe for our early, large productions.

A special thanks for generously opening their homes and sharing their celebrations goes:

To: Joel Dean, Jack Ceglic, Maggie and Jose Hess, Roy Blakey, Joe Lombardo, Mary and Dieter Holterbosch, Heidi and Bruce Addison, Douglas Bushnell and Betty Johnson, Jane and Christopher Johnson, Sheila and Richard Schwartz, and Chuck Hettinger.

For permission to photograph and share their celebrations with our readers, we thank:

Actor's Equity, The Brooklyn Botanic Gardens, Cameron Mackintosh Ltd., Carnegie Hall, The Walt Disney Company, The French Consulate, McNabb and Associates, Merrill-Lynch, The Metropolitan Museum of Art, The Metropolitan Opera, The New York Mercantile Exchange, Paterno Imports, *People Magazine*, Radio City Music Hall, The Really Useful Theatre Company Limited, S.A.G.E., Seagram Classics, and The Victorian Society Scholarship Fund.

To our friends:

Stephen Pool, Barbara Sloan, Jane Hershman, Bob Carlton, Barry Zaid, Fran and Bob Einenkel, Idelle Howitt, Peggy Leak, Jerry Mayro, Gary Carden, Jane Trichter, David Pais, Deirdre Kidder, Barbara Rothberg, and Paul Bernstein, who share our passion for great conversation and great food.

And most of all, we thank our family, who is a constant reminder of the value of celebrating and sharing life's joys.

EVERY TIME WE COMPLETE A PARTY, WE SHARE WITH OUR HOSTS A WONDERFUL SENSE OF ACHIEVEMENT. There is an exuberance that runs through all of our parties. It comes from the fact that we love what we do and we have great fun doing it. With each new experience, we gain greater confidence about our approach and methods. What we have learned we want to share with you.

When we first created our catering company New York Parties, we were intent on capturing the essence of sophisticated New York style for all our events. This turned out to be quite an illusive goal. We spent our early years searching for that one definitive style that would fit every occasion only to discover that styles were as varied as the hosts we met. Style expresses who you are, what you have experienced, and what you enjoy. To host with style is a most luxurious social asset.

In creating our style, we started with the familiar—our own background and ethnic beliefs about food and gracious hosting—and selected what works best for us. We continually explore unfamiliar cultures and uncommon cuisines, and enjoy experimenting with new concepts of music, architecture, decor, and lighting. In every event, the host is always the star. If the production sparkles, the star will shine. We have become producers of an art: the art of hosting.

This book brings that art to you. We have analyzed all the ingredients for planning and hosting wonderful parties. Drawing on fourteen years of experience and hundreds of events, we have included some of our best parties, sharing our secrets, the menus, and recipes. Hosting is fun and it can be easy. Now it is your turn. At the heart of all your parties will be your tastes and your joy. This book invites you to discover your personal style.

"In the midst of winter I finally learned that there
was in me an invincible summer."
—ALBERT CAMUS

JEAN-MICHEL SAVOCA
BOYCE A. BRAWLEY
NEW YORK CITY 1989

The ART of ENTERTAINING

PARTY GIVING IS INDEED AN ART. LIKE ANY IMAGINATIVE ARTIST, YOU WILL COMBINE TALENT, intellect, design, and style to create a successful event. The result will be a joyful expression of your own good taste. Knowing just how to balance serendipitous inspiration with practical skills is the art we want to share with you. This means discovering your own distinctive style and giving it free hand—and then taking a very solid course of action based on careful planning and practical know-how.

Whatever level of involvement you have in mind—from hiring a caterer to do everything, to mixing professional help with do-it-yourself committees, to organizing the entire event and cooking the food yourself—there are certain preliminary guidelines that will ensure a smoothly run and fully attended event. The only ingredient to add is your own sense of style.

Style can exist quietly and privately but to truly flourish it needs a means of expression—entertaining.

General Guidelines

1. Plan every aspect of the party before you extend invitations. Make lists and more lists. Check them off and set your priorities as you go.

2. Make careful projections of the total costs. Decide what your major expenditure will be; cut corners on only the least important items. If, after doing this, you feel you've been unrealistic—the party you envisioned would cost more than you can afford—rethink your plans. If you can't bear to compromise, wait until you can comfortably afford entertaining in the fashion you prefer.

3. If you decide to work with professionals, interview until you find a group that you're comfortable with. Make them aware of all your needs and be sure that they understand your budget and can work within it. Ask for a signed contract that covers every area you discuss and fully outlines your individual responsibilities.

4. Know your guests. Discover their likes and dislikes. Volatile tempers or age-old feuds sometimes subside in convivial surroundings, but they are equally apt to surface.

5. Prepare as much as possible in advance: It is your party, to be done in your style, but that is impossible if you're overburdened with several last-minute details.

6. Dare to be different. When everyone else is going disco, give a Fabulous Fifties Prom. If Chinese is the reigning cuisine, serve fried chicken and grits. Break the formal habit of your social circle by putting together a full-blown peasant picnic.

7. Be prepared for anything. Unexpected disasters are difficult; avoidable ones can and should be prevented.

8. Never discuss how much time, energy, or money has been spent to entertain your guests.

9. Once you are committed to entertaining, be conscious of the value of basic good manners. Common courtesy and thoughtfulness are the most important attributes of a fine host.

Working with a Caterer

Once you have a clear idea of the type of event you wish to host, you must decide if you need professional assistance. This decision is the most important one you'll make during the whole process. Whether you entertain often or are planning a once-in-a-lifetime event, a professional's creative assistance can be indispensable, allowing you the luxury of making the choices without doing the work.

The safest and easiest way to find the right caterer is through recommendations of family, friends, or business associates. But you can easily find resources on your own: Whenever you attend a particularly enjoyable event, always request the caterer's card, and keep it on file with your comments about the party. You should also note caterers mentioned in the social columns of local newspapers and magazines as well as those written about in national publications. Caterers do travel.

No matter what method you use, plan to interview at least three caterers before committing yourself. The interviewing process should begin with a preliminary telephone call, in which you describe the event you're planning. The caterer should review his charge policy and describe how he can make your desires become a reality.

When you feel satisfied that this caterer is someone you might enjoy working with, set up an appointment to visit his office. Seeing his place of business will allow you to assess the professionalism of the operation. The caterer, in some instances, may be the chef; in others, an account executive who works in conjunction with the kitchen and service staffs. You should present a well-defined vision of the event and of your relationship to the guests. Discuss the range of the firm's provisions for full-service catering, from preliminary planning through on-premises clean-up; its creative capabilities in devising themes and decor; its ability to provide service and rental equipment; its charge policy and payment guidelines; and its menu diversity. Ask to view the firm's portfolio and do not hesitate to inquire about any detail you observe in the photographs, reviews, or menus that appear in it. The caterer should offer references and encourage you to contact them, and he should give you a general idea of the budget required. A good caterer may also offer to visit the location of your party to determine how to best use the space. Take advan-

A greenhouse is turned into a formal dining room by our team of professionals.

tage of all the advice and materials presented to you, keeping careful notes.

It is important to be assured that your caterer is properly licensed by local and state agencies and protected by liability insurance. The firm must be able to pay for any damage to your home or rented location, must be insured against any accident involving an intoxicated guest, or any other trauma that might occur. Ask to see copies of their licensing and insurance certificates.

Generally, caterers do not encourage you to visit another client's event or offer tastings from their menus. This is because the professional caterer prefers to keep his full attention on the client of the moment. Occasionally, for large committee-run charitable or corporate functions, a caterer may offer menu samples to speed the final decision.

When the interview is over, you should have a clear idea of the caterer's professionalism and style. Does he have a sense of humor and the ability to take on a disaster when things don't run smoothly

and—most importantly—is he enthusiastic about your project? Once you feel assured, check the volunteered references as a final formality.

After you have selected a caterer, your immediate responsibility is to present your final budget and be explicit about your commitment to it. Is it carved in stone or flexible? If flexible, how much so? Without this information, the caterer is helpless. With it, he can immediately begin to realize your vision.

Allow the caterer a brief period to devise some variations on your theme. Your next meeting will be the time to settle on specifics, so you should use this time to further refine your thoughts as well.

At the second meeting, you will decide together on the theme, the use of your location, the style of service, and any flowers, decorations, or music you would like. The caterer will outline the number and cost of service staff required and the availability and price of rental equipment. You'll set the menu and choose liquors and wines. A sensitive caterer will not infringe his tastes upon yours, but will amplify your choices and expand your imagination. Your enthusiasm can in turn inspire his creativity, resulting in an innovative collaboration. However, keep your enthusiasm within sight of your budget, remembering that ideas cost. A caterer is as much a businessperson as an artist—do not expect to find the "little extras" just thrown in.

After you have agreed on the essential elements, a contract will be drafted. Almost all caterers require a minimum guest count, set by you, which cannot be decreased, with options to increase up to a certain date. The contract will spell out the cost of every detail you have agreed to and outline the payment schedule. A fifty percent deposit is generally required on signing, with the balance due a few days before or on the day of the event. Make very sure that this part of your bargain is clearly understood by both parties.

Learn to say what you mean and mean what you say. Don't be afraid to nix something that you don't like or feel you can't afford. At the same time, be understanding of the caterer's point of view. You are co-creators in this venture.

If the party is to be held in your home or in a borrowed residence, ask the caterer how it can be safeguarded from any damages due to excess. Large numbers of people require oversized cooking pots and other commercial equipment not normally used in a household setting. Make certain that precautions are taken to protect your home from unnecessary wear and tear.

A caterer does not usually get involved with the design or planning of the party invitations, but if you'd like assistance, ask for it. Your caterer may suggest how your invitation can reflect the party's theme. You will need to discuss table arrangements, seating, and place card requirements well in advance. See if your caterer has ideas for special table favors or escort (guest) cards.

Once you have made these decisions, learn to let

The catering staff is there to set the stage for your most important role: A relaxed host or hostess.

go. You have hired a professional who must be free to do his job. He will keep you informed of the progress, and he will not tell you about any complications until after the problem is solved. The initial interview should have assured you that you have found the right person to expand on and fulfill your party dreams. Now is the time to luxuriate in your most important role: a relaxed host or hostess.

On Your Own

If you have the time, energy, and creativity, you can put together a successful party yourself and get a real sense of pride in your work. The same questions you would ask a caterer apply when you decide to handle the party arrangements yourself. Only when you can answer them all satisfactorily are you equipped to stage your own event.

A tight budget, strong creativity, and enthusiastic energy are the most frequent reasons for doing all the work yourself. What you lack in dollars must be made up in time if one person is going to plan, create, chef, and host a successful event for a large number of people. Smaller parties are fairly simple to handle with careful pre-party planning and an easy-to-serve menu.

Sometimes you will be called upon to do volunteer work. If you are part of a committee put together to arrange a benefit, it's wise to select one person to direct. Each committee should be responsible for just one aspect of the event. Call frequent meetings to keep everyone informed of the progress so that nothing lags behind. A well-planned event organized by volunteers can be one of the most enjoyable experiences.

In planning the event, make a careful, informed search to find the appropriate setting, obtain the best food and drink available, hire a helpful staff, and rent reliable equipment. Make sure each firm or person you hire understands your needs, desires, and expectations. Obtain references or samples of their work and examine every bid carefully. Outline all final decisions in contracts and make a pre-party telephone call or visit to confirm your contracted agreement.

Imagination will guide you to the best location for your event.

If you do hire outside assistance, be certain that each person understands exactly what you expect from him before, during, and after the event. We recommend selecting one person from among the service staff to serve as maître d'. Pay him an additional sum to be your right hand, in charge of all other staff and reporting directly to you. If you hire free-lance waiters and waitresses, who generally operate without signed contracts, be sure to agree on the time and method of payment beforehand.

Just as a caterer must be covered by liability insurance, so should you. Check your insurance agent to make certain that your insurance covers any accident that might occur in your home. If you are renting or borrowing a location, find out if the leasor/lender has adequate insurance to cover the use of the location.

Time spent on pre-party planning is an investment that will pay dividends in the form of a successful event. Don't be tempted to take shortcuts.

The ART *of* HOSTING

NEW YORK—THE PARTY MECCA OF THE WORLD, WHERE TRENDS ARE SET AND STYLE IS CREATED—
is our special backdrop, but you can give a New York party anywhere. Whether you're
planning an intimate dinner for two or a rousing banquet for two thousand, you can adapt
New York Parties' distinctive flair to your own environment. We will give you all the guidelines
you need to be a successful host. But whatever you do, you must always be you. If you
aren't comfortable, a plan won't work, even with the help of the best professional caterer.

We have watched many clients bloom as they plan a perfect party. Knowing how to
throw successful parties can open new worlds in your private, business, and charitable lives.
"Party power" lies in the endless opportunity to welcome new people into your orbit. When
you open your home or give a public gathering your distinctive touch, sharing newly
discovered pleasures with old friends and recent acquaintances, you are offering that most
important gift: yourself.

Any entertainment you choose to present should have a warm feeling and bear your
personal stamp. From the inception of New York Parties, this personal involvement of the
host has been the foundation of every party and is, we strongly feel, at the heart of any
successful event. Even if you hire professional help, your own personality and tastes should
give the party a unique quality. Corporate parties and charitable events should carry the

The Grand Tier of The Metropolitan Opera House.

Whether formal or informal, a host always creates a warm inviting atmosphere.

same sense of the sponsor's care for his guests.

Before planning any event, first define its purpose. Try to frame the function by making a list of "givens:" for example, a dinner party to *give* father the chance to be surrounded by his loved ones on his birthday; to *give* our client the opportunity to realize how much we value his business; to *give* our benefactors the opportunity to understand how much their financial and social support has helped our institution. Once you have set the purpose, be clear about your expectations and know your limitations. It helps to review your failures as well as your successes.

A thoughtful host always makes his guests feel welcome and comfortable. That begins with an invitation that clearly states the time, place, and nature of the party, making sure that each guest understands the expected mode of dress. Anticipate any special needs—inquiring about food allergies, for example, or considering the physical comfort of any elderly or disabled guests.

Trust in your ability to bring together a group of convivial people. Mix age groups, cultural backgrounds, and interests if you feel an exciting event will result. If you have created a comfortable atmosphere, the conversation will flow. And you will be relaxed and comfortable, too.

At party time, greet each guest and escort him into the party space. The exception to this rule is for huge corporate or charitable events, when extended staff or committee members may assume the responsibility. If there is a guest of honor, introduce each guest to him, providing some personal information.

Never host any event on a socially competitive basis. If you wish to reciprocate the hospitality of a formal dinner, don't hesitate to plan a barbecue if that best expresses your entertaining style. The best hosts entertain to express their feelings about the guests, not as a venue for self-congratulation or displays of one-upmanship.

The etiquette of a great host is based on understanding the sensibilities of the guests. This is especially important when entertaining strangers, either in your own home or in a corporate atmosphere. If your occasion calls for gifts, arrange for a display area that shows the guests they are appreciated. When an unexpected gift is offered, thank the giver and remove it discretely from view or give it to a service person or close friend to attend to so that you can stay with your guests.

On the day of your party, leave a little time for yourself. Make sure that children are well taken care of and that any minor emergency can be handled without your intervention. Do whatever you must to feel calm and attractive by the time your guests arrive. Dress in a style that is comfortable but does not make you self-conscious. Go through a mental rehearsal and then just let it happen.

As you greet your guests, realize that the party has begun and trust that it will flourish. Spend time with each person, encourage conversation, listen well, smile—don't allow anything to alter your spirits. If you spot a potential mishap or disaster, attend to it quickly and quietly and rejoin your guests. (We've found it helpful to evaluate any crisis as if it were happening to someone else. This kind of objectivity usually produces a solution rather than a panic.)

As host you are expected to keep conversation flowing. Watch for people sitting alone and draw them into the discussion. Your skill at directing conversations will create warm memories of an affair spiced with lively exchanges of anecdotes, information, and friendship.

In your own home, entertaining with style is child's play. Your surroundings are comfortable, you know what to expect, and this feeling will enfold your guests. Just be certain not to invite more guests to your home than you can easily mingle with. Use place cards for dinner parties to ensure that the people you feel will enjoy one another sit together. For buffet dinners, make certain that seating allows comfortable eating and that no one is left to dine alone.

Although corporate entertaining is based on the same principle of pleasing and getting to know more about your guests, it generally has another motive: to extend the business relationship. Objectivity is the key to good corporate hosting; serving

A formal state reception at a consul.

one's personal goals confuses the issue. Business can be carried out, and often is encouraged, at a corporate function.

When acting as a corporate host, make certain that your staff and all service personnel are apprised of the respect due your guests. It is your responsibility to ensure that no awkward moments occur and that the hosting company is seen at its most favorable. Arrive ahead of schedule, arrange seating, greet the guests, and generally create an atmosphere that nurtures business discussion. Be congenial but subdued—a little showmanship will go a long way at corporate functions.

Hosting a fundraiser is yet a different task. Financial goals determine the type of guests invited, and the host must remember that elegance, splendor, power, and prestige are basic elements. A public event should affirm the substance of the organization. It is important that the guest realize his dollars are being used directly to affect the institution. This is the one time to shout and show off. Guests want to stand up and be counted, and they want to do so in the most dazzling surroundings.

Whatever the type of party you plan, if you stick to your goals and concentrate on your guests, you will enjoy yourself, too, knowing that you have brought so much pleasure to others.

A Gala at the Opera

CAVIAR PURSES

FENNEL MOUSSE WITH TOMATO COULIS

LOBSTER WITH TWO VINAIGRETTES

TUSCAN MUSHROOMS WITH ORANGE
VINAIGRETTE

ASPARAGUS WITH RASPBERRY VINAIGRETTE

CHOCOLATE PATE WITH PISTACHIO SAUCE

One of our most glittering galas—an evening called "The Best of the Best"—was a fundraising event held at The Metropolitan Opera House. The evening was organized by a handful of concerned theater people to benefit AIDS research and care. The hosts offered an irresistible combination: a strong commitment to a cause, a stunning location, an array of celebrities to attract ticket buyers, a star-studded show, and a lavish post-performance supper in keeping with the festive spirit. At supper, guests mingled with the performing artists in a celebration of life. Although the cause was serious, the evening was fun and, most importantly, the goal was achieved—in fact, the targeted amount was exceeded.

The Metropolitan Opera House poised for hosting a gala.

Caviar Purses

12 CREPES
½ CUP SOUR CREAM
1 OUNCE BELUGA
    CAVIAR
12 10-INCH-LONG
    SCALLION TIES

SERVES 12

Lay out one crepe at a time and place ½ teaspoon sour cream in the center. Top with about ½ teaspoon caviar, then pull the crepe up around the center to resemble a hobo's bag. Holding the gathered crepe tightly, wrap a scallion tie around it. Tie the scallion into a knot, being careful not to break it. Serve immediately.

*Lacy Crepes bound by
Scallion Ties.*

CREPES

¾ CUP ALL-PURPOSE
    FLOUR
1 EGG
½ CUP MILK
PINCH SALT
⅔ CUP COLD WATER
1½ TABLESPOONS
    MELTED
    UNSALTED
    BUTTER
3 TABLESPOONS
    CLARIFIED BUTTER

Blend the flour, egg, milk, salt, cold water, and melted butter together for 30 seconds in a food processor, using the metal blade. Scrape down the sides of the processor bowl and blend for an additional 30 seconds. Pour mixture into a small mixing bowl. Cover and refrigerate for 1 hour.

Heat a small crepe pan over medium-high heat and brush with enough of the clarified butter to cover the pan's surface. When very hot, but not smoking, lift the pan off the heat and pour in 1½–2 tablespoons of batter. Swirl quickly to cover the bottom of the pan. Return the pan to the heat and cook the crepe for about 1 minute, or until the bottom is cooked and slightly browned. Flip the crepe by shaking the pan gently to free the crepe, then shaking vigorously while at the same time giving the pan a slight twisting upward flip—and cook it about 30 seconds more. Repeat until all the batter is used, stacking the crepes, with waxed paper under each, as you go.

The simple drama of Caviar Purses.

SCALLION TIES

Remove the white ends from the greens and reserve them for another use. Cut the greens along their whole lengths into fine strips or ties. Steam the ties in a vegetable steamer or immerse them in boiling water for 2 seconds. Then lay them out flat separately on waxed paper. Cover and refrigerate until ready to use.

3 SCALLIONS, WITH GREENS AT LEAST 10 INCHES LONG

FENNEL MOUSSE WITH TOMATO COULIS

Butter 12 small egg-shaped molds and line the bottoms with parchment paper (baking paper). Set aside.

Wash and peel the fennel. Finely chop it in a food processor, using the metal blade.

Heat the oil in a medium sauté pan over medium heat. Add the chopped fennel and salt and pepper to taste, and sauté for about 3 minutes, or until wilted. Place the mixture in a small bowl and refrigerate it until well chilled (at least 1 hour). Squeeze the chilled fennel in a towel or cheesecloth, reserving the liquid.

In a food processor, using the metal blade, blend the milk, eggs, and gelatin. Pour this mixture into a small saucepan and cook, stirring constantly, over a low heat for about 4 minutes or until quite thick. Stir in the fennel.

Combine the Pernod and the reserved fennel liquid to make 4 tablespoons. Stir this into the fennel mixture until well combined. Adjust the seasoning to taste.

Whip the heavy cream until stiff. Fold the whipped cream into the fennel mixture and pour the mousse into prepared molds.

Chill for 2 hours, or until set.

To serve, pour the Tomato Coulis onto the bottom of each serving plate and unmold the fennel mousse onto the center. Garnish with a sprinkle of chopped tomato.

2 LARGE HEADS FRESH FENNEL
2 TABLESPOONS EXTRA VIRGIN OLIVE OIL
SALT AND PEPPER TO TASTE
½ CUP MILK
2 LARGE EGGS
2 TEASPOONS UNFLAVORED GELATIN
2 TEASPOONS PERNOD
1 CUP HEAVY CREAM
TOMATO COULIS
1 CUP SEEDED AND CHOPPED TOMATO

SERVES 12

TOMATO COULIS

3¼ POUNDS PLUM TOMATOES
½ CUP OLIVE OIL
2 TABLESPOONS RED WINE VINEGAR

Peel and seed the tomatoes. Place all the ingredients in a food processor and purée until smooth, using the metal blade. Taste and adjust the seasonings.

Chill until ready to serve.

2 TABLESPOONS CHOPPED FRESH ITALIAN PARSLEY
SALT AND PEPPER TO TASTE

LOBSTER WITH TWO VINAIGRETTES

12 1-POUND
    LOBSTERS
1 TABLESPOON SALT
TUSCAN
    MUSHROOMS WITH
    ORANGE
    VINAIGRETTE
ASPARAGUS WITH
    RASPBERRY
    VINAIGRETTE
24 LEMON FLOWERS

SERVES 12

Fill a large stock pot with water and bring it to a boil over high heat. Add salt and lobsters and cook for about 8 minutes, or until the lobsters are bright red and fully cooked. Remove the lobsters from the water, rinse, and drain well. Cool slightly.

Using kitchen shears, neatly cut away the head and fan tail and reserve. Trim the shell from the body, being careful to keep the tail and claw meat whole. Cut the tail meat into medallions, keeping the slices together to preserve the tail shape.

Place each medallioned tail down the center of a 10-inch plate. Set the claw meat on either side of the tail, as it would appear on a whole lobster. Place the head above the medallioned tail and the fan tail below so that you have reassembled a "whole" lobster on the serving plate. Place Tuscan Mushrooms with Orange Vinaigrette on one side of the lobster and Asparagus with Raspberry Vinaigrette on the other. Garnish each with 2 Lemon Flowers.

The key to this lobster dish is presentation.

Tuscan Mushrooms with Orange Vinaigrette

Wash, stem, and dry the mushrooms.

Grate the rind of 2 of the oranges and julienne the rind of the third. Juice all 3 oranges.

Heat the olive oil in a heavy sauté pan over medium heat. Add the minced garlic and sauté it for about 3 minutes, or until almost brown. Add the mushrooms, caps down, and sauté until they begin to wilt. Turn the caps over and sprinkle them with a little cognac. Cook for an additional 2 minutes, then remove the mushrooms.

Deglaze the pan with the remaining cognac. Add the orange juice, grated orange rind, lemon juice, salt and pepper. Reduce the pan juices by one half. Pour them over the mushrooms and let the vinaigrette stand for at least 1 hour before serving. Garnish with julienned orange rind and serve at room temperature.

¼ POUND SHIITAKE MUSHROOMS
3 ORANGES
3 TABLESPOONS OLIVE OIL
1 TABLESPOON MINCED FRESH GARLIC
⅓ CUP COGNAC
½ TEASPOON FRESH LEMON JUICE
SALT AND PEPPER TO TASTE

SERVES 12

Asparagus with Raspberry Vinaigrette

Snap the tough ends off the asparagus. Peel and trim the ends to make them uniform. Bring water to a boil in a large stock pot. Add the salt and asparagus and blanch for about 1 minute, or until the stalks are bright green but still crisp. Drain and transfer them to a bowl of ice water to cover. When they are cool, drain them well and pat dry.

Whisk together the raspberry vinegar and olive oil. Add the salt and pepper to taste and pour the vinaigrette over the dry asparagus. Serve immediately, garnished with fresh raspberries.

60 FRESH, SLIM ASPARAGUS STALKS
½ TEASPOON SALT
¼ CUP RASPBERRY VINEGAR
¾ CUP OLIVE OIL
SALT AND PEPPER TO TASTE
½ PINT FRESH RASPBERRIES

SERVES 12

LEMON FLOWERS

Using a zester or a small sharp paring knife, make cuts running from end to end in the skin of the lemon about ⅛-inch deep, no more than ¼-inch wide, and no more than ½-inch apart.

Slice the lemons crosswise ⅛- to ¼-inch thick to make uniform lemon "flowers." Use as a garnish.

4 LARGE UNBLEMISHED THICK-SKINNED LEMONS

CHOCOLATE PATE WITH PISTACHIO SAUCE

16 OUNCES
  SEMISWEET
  CHOCOLATE
2 CUPS CONFEC-
  TIONERS' SUGAR
1½ CUPS UNSALTED
  BUTTER
10 LARGE EGGS,
  SEPARATED
1½ CUPS
  UNSWEETENED
  COCOA POWDER
PINCH SALT
¼ TEASPOON CREAM
  OF TARTAR
1½ CUPS HEAVY
  CREAM
PISTACHIO SAUCE
½ CUP TOASTED
  CHOPPED
  PISTACHIOS

SERVES 12

Melt the chocolate in the top of a double boiler over very hot water. Add the sugar and mix well. Whisk in the butter, one piece at a time, until blended. Remove the pan from over the water and whisk in the egg yolks one at a time, mixing well after each addition. Whisk in the cocoa. Cool for 5 minutes, stirring frequently.

Beat the egg whites with the salt and cream of tartar until soft peaks form. Gently stir one-third of the whites into the chocolate mixture; then fold in the remaining whites. Do not beat.

Whip the heavy cream until soft peaks form and carefully fold the whipped cream into the chocolate mixture.

Pour the batter into a pâté mold, cover, and chill for at least 12 hours. Just before serving, moisten a kitchen towel with hot water and wrap it around the mold. Invert the mold and gently shake the pâté out. Pour Pistachio Sauce onto each serving plate, spreading it to coat the entire surface. Using a serrated knife, cut the pâté into ¼-inch slices. Place a pâté slice in the center of the sauce, dribble a bit of sauce on top, and sprinkle with toasted chopped pistachios. Serve immediately.

PISTACHIO SAUCE

1 CUP SHELLED
  PISTACHIOS
2½ CUPS MILK
1 TEASPOON
  VANILLA EXTRACT
10 EGG YOLKS
¾ CUP SUGAR
PINCH SALT
⅓ CUP PISTACHIO
  LIQUEUR

Place the pistachios in a small saucepan. Cover them with water and bring to a boil over high heat. Lower the heat and cook for about 4 minutes, or until soft. Drain well. Peel the skins from the nuts and pat them dry. Grind and reserve.

Place the milk and vanilla extract in a non-reactive pan over medium heat and cook until the milk begins to scald.

Combine the yolks, sugar, and salt in the bowl of an electric mixer and beat until pale yellow and thick. Slowly beat one cup of the heated milk into the yolk mixture and then pour the yolk mixture into the remaining milk in the saucepan, whisking constantly. Cook the custard over medium heat, stirring constantly, until thickened. Do not boil.

Add the ground pistachios and pistachio liqueur to the custard. Cover and refrigerate until ready to use.

The richness of the dessert should reflect the splendor of the surroundings.

Cocktails at the Consul

SHRIMP DIJON

ESCARGOT EN COQUILLE

FOIE GRAS WITH PAPAYA

STEAK AND AVOCADO TARTARE

WILD MUSHROOMS IN PHYLLO PASTRY

CHEVRE AND LEEK PASTIES

CAVIAR IN TART SHELLS

An official reception is the ultimate reflection of a country's culture. The host represents his government and people in a most gracious manner at a conspicuous setting, highlighting the mutual respect between guest and host, and encouraging communication. Here protocol and placement are paramount to ensure that each guest has the opportunity to meet the host and to impart his or her message. Grandeur and pomp are important elements, but the line into ostentation is never crossed. For this reception, the host served only champagne with a light and sophisticated menu that complemented the sparkling drink.

A formal spring bouquet sets the mood for an official reception.

SHRIMP DIJON

¾ POUND SHRIMP, COOKED, SHELLED, AND DEVEINED

⅓ CUP DIJON MUSTARD

2 TABLESPOONS CHOPPED FRESH SHALLOTS

1 TABLESPOON CHOPPED FRESH ITALIAN PARSLEY

In a food processor, using the metal blade, mix together the mustard, shallots, parsley, vinegars, oil, and red pepper flakes. When the mixture is well blended, pour it over the cooked shrimp.

Cover and refrigerate the shrimp for at least 2 hours. When you are ready to serve it, stir and place each shrimp on a toothpick.

1 TABLESPOON RED WINE VINEGAR

1 TABLESPOON WHITE WINE VINEGAR

¼ CUP OLIVE OIL

PINCH RED PEPPER FLAKES

SERVES 12

Shrimp with a piquant Dijon vinaigrette.

NOTE: THE QUANTITIES FOR THESE RECIPES ARE BASED ON ONE SERVING PER PERSON, BUT CAN BE DOUBLED.

ESCARGOT EN COQUILLE

12 CANNED SNAILS, RINSED AND DRAINED

¼ CUP SALTED BUTTER

1 TABLESPOON CHOPPED FRESH SHALLOTS

1 TABLESPOON CHOPPED FRESH GARLIC

1 TABLESPOON FRESH ITALIAN PARSLEY

Preheat the oven to 375°.

In a food processor, using the metal blade, beat the salted butter until very soft. Add the shallots, garlic, parsley, Pernod, and pepper and blend well. Remove the garlic butter from the bowl, cover, and chill.

Drop the broccoli florets in boiling water for about 15 seconds. Immediately remove them to a bowl of ice water. When they are well chilled, drain and pat them dry.

Prepare Tart Dough and bake the 12 mini-tart shells. Allow them to cool thoroughly. Place a broccoli floret in the hollow of each. Place a small piece of unsalted butter on top of the floret, add one snail, and finish with ¼ teaspoon of the garlic butter.

Place the tarts on a baking sheet and bake for about 2 minutes, or until the snails are heated through and the butter is bubbling. Serve hot.

¼ TEASPOON PERNOD

PEPPER TO TASTE

12 BROCCOLI FLORETS

TART DOUGH

2 TABLESPOONS UNSALTED BUTTER

SERVES 12

TART DOUGH
(Traditional Method)

Sift the flour, then sift it again with the salt. Cut half of the short-enings into the flour with a pastry blender (or work it lightly with your fingers) until the mixture is mealy. Cut the remaining short-enings coarsely into the dough until the pieces are pea size.

Sprinkle the dough with some of the water and blend lightly with a fork, adding just enough water to hold the ingredients together. When the dough can be gathered into a ball, immediately stop handling it. Wrap it in plastic wrap and refrigerate for 12 hours or more.

Preheat the oven to 425°.

Roll out the dough ⅛-inch thick on a lightly floured board and cut it into circles large enough to line the mini-tart pans (or large tart or pie pans). Do not grease the pans. Weight each tart with pastry weights, beans, or rice, and bake them for 8 minutes (or 12 minutes, if you are baking a large tart or pie shell), or until golden. Allow to cool in the pans.

2 CUPS SIFTED ALL-PURPOSE FLOUR
1 TEASPOON SALT
⅓ CUP UNSALTED MARGARINE
⅓ CUP CHILLED UNSALTED BUTTER
5 TABLESPOONS COLD WATER

MAKES PASTRY FOR 12 MINI-TART SHELLS OR A 2-CRUST PIE

TART DOUGH
(Food Processor Method)

The tart shell transforms this classic first course into an hors d'oeuvre.

Put the butter, margarine, flour, and salt into the bowl of a food processor. Using the metal blade, blend for 2 seconds. Add the ice water a little at a time, with the machine running, until the dough pulls away from the sides of the bowl and forms a ball. Wrap the dough in plastic wrap and refrigerate it for at least 1 hour to allow dough to rest.

Preheat the oven to 425°.

Roll out the dough ⅛-inch thick on a lightly floured board and cut it into the desired shape(s) as described in the traditional method. Bake for 8 minutes (for mini-tart shells) or for 12 minutes (for a large tart or pie shells), or until golden. Allow to cool in the pans.

2 TABLESPOONS UNSALTED BUTTER
3 TABLESPOONS UNSALTED MARGARINE
1⅓ CUPS ALL-PURPOSE FLOUR
¼ TEASPOON SALT
¼ CUP ICE WATER

MAKES PASTRY FOR 12 MINI-TART SHELLS OR A 2-CRUST PIE

Papaya adds an exotic touch to foie gras.

FOIE GRAS WITH PAPAYA

12 1½ X1-INCH RECTANGLES FROM GOOD-QUALITY WHITE BREAD (ABOUT 4–6 SLICES)

1½ TABLESPOONS CLARIFIED BUTTER

¼ POUND FOIE GRAS (BLOCK)

½ FRESH PAPAYA

SERVES 12

Preheat the oven to 350°.

Place the bread rectangles on a baking sheet and bake them for about 3 minutes, or until lightly toasted. Immediately brush them with the clarified butter.

Cut rectangles of foie gras exactly to fit on top of the toasts.

Cut the papaya into thin slices and cut the slices into 24 small diamonds. Place a papaya diamond on top of each piece of foie gras. Serve immediately.

In place of papaya, you can use mango for Foie Gras with Mango.

Steak tartare studded with avocado.

STEAK AND AVOCADO TARTARE

⅓ POUND EXTRA
   LEAN GROUND
   SIRLOIN
1 LARGE EGG YOLK
1 TABLESPOON
   CAPERS
2 TABLESPOONS
   WORCESTERSHIRE
   SAUCE
½ TEASPOON OLIVE
   OIL
¼ MEDIUM RIPE
   AVOCADO
2 ANCHOVY FILLETS

Place the beef in a mixing bowl. Add the egg yolk, capers, Worcestershire sauce, and olive oil. Mix gently.

In a food processor, using the metal blade, chop the avocado, anchovy fillets, 1 tablespoon of the parsley, and the onion. Add this mixture to the beef and stir just to blend. Add salt and pepper to taste.

Place a heaping mound of tartare on each pumpernickel circle and garnish with the remaining chopped parsley.

Serve immediately.

2 TABLESPOONS
   CHOPPED FRESH
   ITALIAN PARSLEY
2 TABLESPOONS
   CHOPPED ONION
SALT AND PEPPER
   TO TASTE
12 1½-INCH
   DIAMETER
   PUMPERNICKEL
   BREAD CIRCLES
   (ABOUT 4–6 SLICES)

SERVES 12

WILD MUSHROOMS IN PHYLLO PASTRY

¼ POUND FRESH
   WILD MUSHROOMS
   (OR FRESH
   MUSHROOMS)
1 STALK CELERY
1 TABLESPOON
   OLIVE OIL
1 TABLESPOON
   FINELY CHOPPED
   ONION
PINCH DRIED
   GROUND
   ROSEMARY
PINCH DRIED
   GROUND THYME

In a food processor, using the metal blade, finely chop the mushrooms. Set them aside. Finely chop the celery and set it aside.

Heat the olive oil in a sauté pan over medium heat. When it is hot, add the onion and sauté it for 3 minutes, or until wilted. Add the celery, rosemary, and thyme and sauté for an additional 2 minutes. Stir in the mushrooms and cook until slightly soft. Add the vinegar, cognac, and salt and pepper to taste. Continue cooking until the liquid has evaporated.

Remove the mixture from the heat and blend in enough bread crumbs to hold the filling together. Adjust the seasonings to taste. Fill and form 12 small phyllo triangles, following the directions on the package of the commercially prepared dough. Bake them as directed.

Serve warm.

1 TEASPOON RED
   WINE VINEGAR
1 TEASPOON
   COGNAC
SALT AND PEPPER
   TO TASTE
2 TABLESPOONS
   FRESH BREAD
   CRUMBS
¼ PACKAGE
   COMMERCIAL
   PHYLLO DOUGH

SERVES 12

CHEVRE AND LEEK PASTIES

1 FRESH LEEK, WHITE
   PART ONLY
1 TABLESPOON
   OLIVE OIL
¼ POUND BUCHERON
   (GOAT CHEESE)
3 TABLESPOONS
   SEASONED BREAD
   CRUMBS
1 TABLESPOON
   COGNAC

Preheat the oven to 375°.

Wash the leek thoroughly. Pat it dry and chop into small pieces.

Heat the olive oil in a small sauté pan over medium heat. When hot, add the leek and sauté for about 3 minutes, or until soft.

Beat the Bucheron on high speed with an electric mixer until very smooth. Fold in the leeks, bread crumbs, cognac, rosemary, and salt and pepper to taste. Place a teaspoonful of cheese into the center of each Tart Dough circle. Fold the circle in half and seal the edges by wetting them a bit and pressing the edges with the tines of a fork to finish.

Beat the egg yolk. Place the pasties on an ungreased baking sheet and brush them lightly with beaten egg yolk. Bake for 8 minutes, or until lightly browned. Serve warm.

PINCH DRIED
   GROUND
   ROSEMARY
SALT AND PEPPER
   TO TASTE
12 2½-INCH TART
   DOUGH CIRCLES
   (SEE PAGE 29)
1 EGG YOLK

SERVES 12

CAVIAR IN TART SHELLS

3 OUNCES BELUGA
   CAVIAR

Using a non-reactive spoon, place a generous heap of caviar into a baked mini-tart shell. Serve immediately.

12 BAKED MINI-TART
   SHELLS (SEE PAGE
   29)

SERVES 12

Caviar and champagne give any event an elegant and formal tone.

A Townhouse Christmas

CHRISTMAS PUNCH

CHEDDAR WAFERS

STUFFED DATES

ROAST GOOSE WITH APPLE STUFFING

SMITHFIELD HAM WITH RED-EYE GRAVY

SHERRIED YAMS

WILD RICE PILAF

BUTTERMILK BISCUITS

PICKLED SHALLOTS

GLAZED WINTER VEGETABLES

BREAD PUDDING WITH BOURBON SAUCE

OLD-FASHIONED SUGAR COOKIES

We created "A Townhouse Christmas" for a California vintner as part of its annual corporate thank-you to the top wine producers. A weekend in New York City, filled with shopping and theater, was topped off with a glittering New York–style family Christmas dinner. Such an event required the most spectacular location and decor—a townhouse on Park Avenue filled with a twinkling Christmas tree swathed in gold and silver. It was a perfect way for the host to show its delight in and appreciation for the guests, and it stimulated a commitment to excellence for the coming year.

The inviting sparkle of Park Avenue at Christmas.

An aroma of a hot Christmas Punch greets guests as they enter the party.

CHRISTMAS PUNCH

12 CUPS PINEAPPLE
  JUICE
4 CUPS APRICOT
  NECTAR
5 CUPS APPLE CIDER

Combine all the ingredients in a large, non-reactive saucepan over medium heat. Bring to a simmer; then lower the heat and cook for 10 minutes. Strain the punch and serve hot.

3 CUPS FRESH
  ORANGE JUICE
8 CINNAMON STICKS
20 WHOLE CLOVES

SERVES 12

CHEDDAR WAFERS

4 TABLESPOONS
  MARGARINE
¼ POUND GRATED
  SHARP CHEDDAR
PINCH CAYENNE
  PEPPER
PINCH SALT
DASH TABASCO
  SAUCE

In the bowl of an electric mixer, cream the margarine and grated cheddar. When it is smooth, add the cayenne pepper, salt, and Tabasco sauce.

Blend in the flour in small amounts to make a firm dough. Chill the dough for about 1 hour.

Preheat the oven to 325°.

Roll the dough out to ¼-inch thickness and cut it into circles with a 1½-inch biscuit cutter. Place a tiny piece of crystallized ginger in the center of each wafer. Place them on an ungreased baking sheet and bake for 10 minutes. Sprinkle the wafers with sugar while they are still warm. Serve at room temperature.

½ CUP ALL-PURPOSE
  FLOUR
24 TINY PIECES
  CRYSTALLIZED
  GINGER
2 TABLESPOONS
  SUGAR

MAKES 24

STUFFED DATES

½ CUP CREAM
CHEESE,
SOFTENED

2 TEASPOONS
FROZEN ORANGE
JUICE
CONCENTRATE

½ TEASPOON
ORANGE EXTRACT
(OR 1 TABLESPOON
GRATED FRESH
ORANGE RIND)

Blend the cream cheese, juice concentrate, and extract (or rind).
Add the nuts.

Using a small spoonful of cheese mixture, stuff each date. Chill,
then roll them in the confectioners' sugar. Cover and refrigerate
the dates until you are ready to serve them.

⅔ CUP CHOPPED
PECANS

1 POUND PITTED
DATES

½ CUP
CONFECTIONERS'
SUGAR

MAKES 24

ROAST GOOSE
WITH APPLE STUFFING

1 24-POUND FRESH
GOOSE

4 POUNDS DRIED
CHESTNUTS

4 CUPS FRESH
CHICKEN STOCK

1 TEASPOON SUGAR

PINCH SALT

½ POUND BACON

1 ½ CUPS CHOPPED
FRESH CELERY

3 CUPS CHOPPED
ONION

¼ CUP CHOPPED
FRESH ITALIAN
PARSLEY

½ TEASPOON DRIED
GROUND
ROSEMARY

Preheat the oven to 450°.

Wash the goose and dry it thoroughly. Lightly salt and pepper
the cavity and place the goose on a roasting rack.

Place the chestnuts and Chicken Stock in a heavy saucepan
over medium heat. Add the sugar and a pinch of salt. Bring the
mixture to a boil. Cover it and lower the heat. Simmer for 1 hour,
or until the chestnuts are softened but not mushy. Remove the
chestnuts from the stock and reserve both.

Cut the bacon into small pieces and place them in a heavy
frying pan over low heat. Cook for 15 minutes, or until the bacon
is crisp. Drain the bacon on a paper towel, reserving 3 tablespoons
of fat in the pan. Add the celery, onion, parsley, and rosemary
and cook over low heat until the vegetables are wilted.

Peel, core, and dice the apples. Melt the butter in a non-reactive
sauté pan. Add the diced apples, lemon juice, and Calvados. Sauté
for 5 minutes. Combine the vegetable and apple mixtures with
the bread cubes, using reserved Chicken Stock to moisten as
necessary to bind the stuffing together. Add salt and pepper to
taste.

Stuff the goose cavity and sew up the opening. Combine the
apple juice and soy sauce and brush it on the goose. Cook for 3
hours, or until a meat thermometer registers 185°, basting frequently with the apple juice/soy sauce mixture. Place on a platter
and serve immediately.

10 GRANNY SMITH
APPLES (OR ANY
GREEN APPLE)

½ CUP UNSALTED
BUTTER

¼ CUP FRESH LEMON
JUICE

1 TABLESPOON
CALVADOS

4 CUPS FRESH HOME-
STYLE BREAD
CUBES

SALT AND PEPPER
TO TASTE

½ CUP APPLE JUICE

½ CUP LIGHT SOY
SAUCE

SERVES 12

CHICKEN STOCK

4 POUNDS CHICKEN
PARTS (WINGS,
NECKS, BACKS)

2 QUARTS COLD
WATER

4 SPRIGS FRESH
ITALIAN PARSLEY

4 SPRIGS FRESH DILL
(1 TEASPOON DRIED
DILL)

Place all of the ingredients in a stock pot. Bring them to a boil.
Reduce the heat to simmer and cook for approximately 2 ½ hours
or until the liquid is reduced by half. Skim the surface of any
foam or residue.

Strain the stock through a double layer of cheese cloth. Discard
all of the solid ingredients. Cool.

2 BAY LEAVES

1 TEASPOON BLACK
PEPPERCORNS

1 CHOPPED ONION

3 CARROTS, PEELED
AND CHOPPED

4 CELERY STALKS,
WASHED AND
CHOPPED

4 CLOVES GARLIC

Roast Goose with Apple Stuffing and Smithfield Ham are traditional Christmas favorites.

SMITHFIELD HAM WITH RED-EYE GRAVY

The family tree.

Place the ham in a deep pot, cover it with cold water, and let it stand for 12 hours.

Pour off the water, rinse the ham, and place it in the same pot, skin side down. Cover it with cold water and bring to a boil over high heat. Lower the heat, cover, and simmer for 20 minutes per pound.

Remove the pot from the heat. Uncover it and allow the ham to sit in the cooking liquid until cool. Remove it from the liquid and wipe off the excess moisture.

Preheat the oven to 400°.

Place the ham on a rack, fat side up, in a roasting pan. Trim off the top skin and some of the fat. Sprinkle the ham with the ground cinnamon, ground cloves, and allspice. Blend together the brown sugar, bread crumbs, and pineapple juice or sherry. When this is well mixed, use it to coat the surface of the ham, packing it down firmly. Stud the top of the ham with the whole cloves. Bake it for about 20 minutes, or until the top is golden. Reserve the drippings in the pan, if you plan to make gravy.

To serve, slice the ham very thin. If serving hot, drizzle Red-Eye Gravy over the slices.

1 15-POUND SMITHFIELD HAM
1 TABLESPOON GROUND CINNAMON
1 TABLESPOON GROUND CLOVES
1 TABLESPOON GROUND ALLSPICE
1 CUP LIGHT BROWN SUGAR, TIGHTLY PACKED
½ CUP FINE BREAD CRUMBS
2 TABLESPOONS, PINEAPPLE JUICE (OR DRY SHERRY)
2 TABLESPOONS WHOLE CLOVES
RED-EYE GRAVY

SERVES 12 OR MORE

RED-EYE GRAVY

Pour the coffee into the ham roasting pan. Place the pan over medium heat and bring the gravy to a boil, stirring constantly. Continue boiling for about 8 minutes, or until all the roasting residue has been scraped from the pan and the flavors have combined. Serve hot, drizzled over sliced ham.

PAN DRIPPINGS FROM SMITHFIELD HAM
3½ CUPS STRONG BLACK COFFEE

SHERRIED YAMS

18 SMALL YAMS
⅓ CUP UNSALTED BUTTER
⅔ CUP DARK CORN SYRUP

In a saucepan over medium heat, boil the yams until tender. Cool them slightly and peel.

Melt the butter in a heavy sauté pan over medium heat. Stir in the corn syrup, cinnamon, and sherry. When the mixture is well blended, add the cooked yams. Cook, turning frequently, until the liquid has caramelized on the yams. Serve immediately.

1 TEASPOON GROUND CINNAMON
⅓ CUP DRY SHERRY

SERVES 12

WILD RICE PILAF

⅓ CUP BUTTER
½ CUP DICED CELERY
½ CUP DICED ONION
2 CUPS WILD RICE
3 CUPS FRESH
   CHICKEN STOCK
   (SEE PAGE 37)

Melt the butter in a saucepan over medium heat. Add the diced celery and onion and sauté for 5 minutes. Add the rice and cook for approximately 2 minutes, or until the rice is well coated. Add the stock and cook for 45 minutes, or until the stock is absorbed. Remove the rice from the heat. Add the diced red pepper and the water chestnuts. Adjust the seasonings and serve immediately.

1 RED PEPPER,
   SEEDED AND
   DICED
¾ CUP SLICED WATER
   CHESTNUTS
SALT AND PEPPER
   TO TASTE

SERVES 12

An unusual pilaf made with wild rice.

BUTTERMILK BISCUITS

2 CUPS
   ALL-PURPOSE
   FLOUR
½ TEASPOON SALT
1 TABLESPOON
   SUGAR
2 TABLESPOONS
   BAKING POWDER

Preheat the oven to 375°.

Sift all the dry ingredients together. Cut in the shortening and add just enough buttermilk to moisten. Mix with your hands to make a soft dough.

Roll out the dough on a lightly floured board and fold it once. Roll it out again ½-inch thick and cut it into biscuits of the desired size. Place the biscuits on an ungreased cookie sheet and bake them for 15 minutes, or until light brown. Serve warm.

¼ TEASPOON BAKING
   SODA
3 TABLESPOONS
   VEGETABLE
   SHORTENING
⅔ CUP BUTTERMILK

MAKES 24

PICKLED SHALLOTS

Pour enough boiling water over the shallots to cover them. Let stand for 2 hours, then peel the shallots.

Mix 1 tablespoon of the salt into enough cold water to cover the peeled shallots. Pour the salted water over the shallots in a non-metallic container. Cover and let them stand overnight.

Pour the brine off the shallots. Mix another tablespoon of salt with cold water and pour over the shallots, as above. Cover and let them stand another night.

Pour off the brine and repeat the process, using the last table-spoon of salt.

Pour off the brine and rinse the shallots in cold running water for 5 minutes.

Bring the vinegar, sugar, celery seed, and mustard seed to a boil. Place half of the shallots and peppers into each of 2 sterilized containers and cover with boiling syrup. Cover and seal at once. Let them rest 12 hours before using.

2 PINTS SHALLOTS
3 TABLESPOONS NON-IODIZED SALT
½ RED PEPPER, SLICED
½ GREEN PEPPER, SLICED
1 CUP WHITE VINEGAR
½ CUP SUGAR
½ TEASPOON CELERY SEED
½ TEASPOON MUSTARD SEED

MAKES 2 PINTS

GLAZED WINTER VEGETABLES

The bounty of winter vegetables presents a palette of earthy hues.

Peel the turnips, carrots, and beets. Be certain to keep the beets separate so that they don't discolor the other vegetables. Remove the outer leaves from the Brussels sprouts and the outer skin from the pearl onions. Score the bottoms of the Brussels sprouts with an X.

"Turn" the turnip, zucchini, yellow squash, carrots, and beets into pieces comparable in size to the Brussels sprouts.

Place all the vegetables except the beets in a sauté pan. Cook them over medium heat with most of the butter, sugar, and salt to taste. Cook the beets and the remaining butter, sugar, and salt in a separate pan. Cover all the vegetables by half with the Chicken Stock, simmer covered, for about 10 minutes, or until cooked.

Remove the lid and reduce the glaze by half, shaking the pan often to prevent the vegetables from sticking.

Serve immediately.

1 POUND TURNIPS
½ POUND CARROTS
½ POUND FRESH BEETS
1 POUND BRUSSELS SPROUTS
½ POUND WHITE PEARL ONIONS
3 ZUCCHINI SQUASHES
3 YELLOW SQUASHES
¼ CUP SALTED BUTTER
2 TABLESPOONS SUGAR
PINCH SALT
1 CUP FRESH CHICKEN STOCK (SEE PAGE 37)

SERVES 12

BREAD PUDDING
WITH BOURBON SAUCE

½ CUP YELLOW
RAISINS
1 CUP BOILING
WATER
1 ¼ CUP SUGAR
2 LARGE EGGS
1 TABLESPOON
VANILLA EXTRACT
1 ⅔ CUPS MILK
⅔ CUP UNSALTED
BUTTER
1 2-INCH PIECE
VANILLA BEAN
1 LARGE FRENCH
BAGUETTE
BOURBON SAUCE

SERVES 12

Preheat the oven to 400°.

Cover the raisins with the boiling water and let them set until well plumped. Drain the raisins and reserve them.

Whisk together the sugar, eggs, and vanilla until well blended.

Heat the milk, butter, and vanilla bean in a small saucepan over medium heat until just scalded. Whisk the milk mixture into the egg mixture. Add the raisins.

Cut the baguette into cubes and toss the cubes in the egg custard until well coated.

Butter a 2 x 9 x 12-inch baking dish and pour in the bread mixture. Place the dish in a larger pan filled halfway with water. Bake for about 45 minutes, or until the top of the pudding is light brown and slightly puffed. Serve warm, with Bourbon Sauce.

BOURBON SAUCE

⅔ CUP WARM MELTED
UNSALTED
BUTTER
½ CUP SUGAR

Mix all the ingredients in a blender until well combined. Serve immediately.

2 LARGE EGGS
⅓ CUP BOURBON

OLD-FASHIONED SUGAR COOKIES

1 CUP UNSALTED
BUTTER
1 ¼ CUPS SUGAR
2 LARGE EGGS
1 TEASPOON
VANILLA
2 ½ CUPS
ALL-PURPOSE
FLOUR
SCANT ½ TEASPOON
BAKING SODA
½ CUP SILVER
DRAGEES

SERVES 12

Cream the butter and 1 cup of the sugar until light and fluffy. Add the eggs and beat until blended. Stir in the vanilla. Sift the flour and soda together and stir into the dough. Cover and refrigerate for several hours or overnight.

Preheat the oven to 350°.

Roll out a small portion of dough at a time on a lightly floured board to no more than ⅛-inch thick. Cut it into desired shapes and place them on a greased cookie sheet. Sprinkle the cookies with the remaining sugar and bake for 10 minutes, or until just golden. Cool on wire racks. Garnish each cookie with a silver dragee as it cools.

Bread Pudding with Bourbon Sauce and Old-fashioned Sugar Cookies.

A Thai Dinner at Home

CURRIED SCALLOPS WITH BASIL

FILET MIGNON WITH PEANUT SAUCE

THAI ROASTED CHICKEN

SEASONED CUCUMBERS

GREEN PAPAYA SALAD

SHRIMP AND LEMON GRASS SOUP

STRING BEANS WITH FRESH GINGER

POMELO SALAD

TARO AND CELERY ROOT CHIPS

TAKAW

A Thai feast was created to highlight the atmosphere of this host's home, which was filled with Thai antiques, and Oriental souvenirs. His parties are always successful because they reflect the spirit of *sanuk*, or abundant hospitality. He shares his exotic interests with his guests. For old friends, his home is a familiar and comfortably enveloping setting; for new ones, it can be a vivid introduction to the Orient.

The evening began with stories, Thai street food, and soup served on a low table. Guests kicked off their shoes and eased into the fascinating conversation. Dinner was staged on a dining platform from which each guest could view the beautiful artifacts that filled every corner of the living room. Once dinner had ended, it was back to the low tables and sofas for coffee, Thai desserts, and more stories. The evening immersed the guests in another time and place. Charmed by hospitality and a bit of culture shock—they couldn't wait to be invited back.

Private celebrations at home reflect personal tastes.
OVERLEAF *A Thai buffet is a delicate balance of familiar and exotic flavors.*

CURRIED SCALLOPS WITH BASIL

2 POUNDS SCALLOPS

2 TEASPOONS MILD CURRY POWDER

1 LARGE RED PEPPER

3 TABLESPOONS OLIVE OIL

2 TABLESPOONS CHILI OIL

2 TABLESPOONS CHOPPED FRESH GARLIC

3 TABLESPOONS NAM PLA (ORIENTAL FISH SAUCE)*

30 LARGE BASIL LEAVES

SERVES 12

Rinse the scallops and score each with a cross hatch on top. Sprinkle them with curry powder and set aside.

Wash, seed, and julienne the red pepper.

Heat 1 teaspoon of the olive oil in a sauté pan over low heat. Add the julienned red pepper and sauté for 2 minutes, or until just wilted. Set aside and keep warm.

Add the chili oil and the remaining olive oil to a sauté pan. Stir in the chopped garlic and sauté for 3 minutes, or until the garlic is almost brown.

Remove the garlic with a slotted spoon and add the scallops, scored side down. This will cause the scallops to open into a flower shape. Sauté for 2 minutes; then add the Nam Pla. Cook for an additional 2 minutes.

Place the basil leaves on a serving platter and top each with a flowered scallop. Garnish with the julienned red peppers.

NOTE: INGREDIENTS MARKED WITH AN AS-TERISK (*) CAN BE FOUND IN THE ORIEN-TAL SECTIONS OF MOST SUPERMAR-KETS, SPECIALTY STORES, AND ORIEN-TAL MARKETS.

Curried scallops seared to golden perfection.

FILET MIGNON WITH PEANUT SAUCE

1½ POUNDS FILET MIGNON

½ TEASPOON FINELY GROUND BLACK PEPPER

1½ TABLESPOONS WORCESTERSHIRE SAUCE

6 TABLESPOONS SMOOTH PEANUT BUTTER

¼ CUP SOY SAUCE

Cube the filet mignon and combine it with the black pepper and Worcestershire sauce. Let it marinate for at least 1 hour.

In a food processor, using the metal blade, combine the peanut butter, soy sauce, lemon juice, red pepper flakes, and heavy cream. Remove this sauce from the bowl and set aside.

Heat the butter in a heavy sauté pan over high heat. Add the filet and sauté for 2 minutes, or until seared but still rare.

Serve the filet cubes warm with peanut sauce and Seasoned Cucumbers on the side.

2½ TEASPOONS FRESH LEMON JUICE

1 TEASPOON RED PEPPER FLAKES

¾ CUP HEAVY CREAM

2 TABLESPOONS UNSALTED BUTTER

SEASONED CUCUMBERS

SERVES 12

The combination of lemon grass and coconut milk gives Thai Roasted Chicken its unique flavor.

THAI ROASTED CHICKEN

6 WHOLE CHICKEN
  BREASTS
6 CHICKEN THIGHS
6 CHICKEN LEGS
4 STALKS LEMON
  GRASS, CUT INTO
  PIECES*
2 TABLESPOONS
  MINCED FRESH
  GINGER ROOT
½ CUP CHOPPED
  FRESH SHALLOTS
1 CUP CHOPPED
  FRESH PARSNIP

Wash the chicken pieces. Split the breasts and trim off any cartilage. Pat all the pieces dry and set them aside in a large bowl.

In a food processor, using the metal blade, combine the lemon grass, ginger root, shallots, parsnip, brown sugar, cream of coconut, Nam Pla, soy sauce, and oil. Blend until smooth.

Pour the sauce over the chicken. Cover and refrigerate for at least 8 hours.

Preheat the oven to 350°.

Place the chicken pieces on baking sheets and cook for 35 minutes, or until golden brown. Serve garnished with the chopped coriander.

⅓ CUP LIGHT BROWN
  SUGAR, TIGHTLY
  PACKED
1 CUP SWEETENED
  CREAM OF
  COCONUT
¼ CUP NAM PLA
  (ORIENTAL FISH
  SAUCE)*
¼ CUP LIGHT SOY
  SAUCE
¼ CUP CORN OIL
½ CUP CHOPPED
  FRESH CORIANDER
  (CILANTRO)

SERVES 12

SEASONED CUCUMBERS

3 LARGE
  CUCUMBERS
¾ CUP CHOPPED
  SHALLOTS
½ CUP SUGAR
¾ CUP RICE WINE
  VINEGAR*
¾ CUP COLD WATER

Peel and slice the cucumbers paper thin. Place them in a shallow dish and sprinkle them with the chopped shallots.

In a medium saucepan, over high heat, combine the sugar, vinegar, and water. Stir to blend and cook, stirring frequently, until reduced by half. Immediately pour the mixture over the cucumbers.

When the cucumbers are cool, toss in the chopped coriander and mint. Add salt to taste and serve at room temperature.

3 TABLESPOONS
  CHOPPED FRESH
  CORIANDER
  (CILANTRO)
3 TABLESPOONS
  CHOPPED FRESH
  MINT
SALT TO TASTE

SERVES 12

GREEN PAPAYA SALAD

3 TABLESPOONS MINCED GARLIC

1 FRESH RED CHILI PEPPER, SEEDED AND DEVEINED

⅓ CUP PEANUT OIL

¼ CUP RICE WINE VINEGAR*

3 TABLESPOONS SOY SAUCE

½ CUP FRESH LIME JUICE

In a food processor, using the metal blade, combine the garlic, chili pepper, oil, rice wine vinegar, soy sauce, and lime juice until well blended. Remove the dressing from the processor bowl and set aside.

Peel and seed the papayas. Cut them into a fine julienne.

Wash and peel the tomatoes and slice them into thin slices.

Wash, trim, and dry the lettuce leaves and place them on a serving platter. Mound the papaya in the center and circle it with the tomato slices. Sprinkle the papaya with cayenne pepper and drizzle the dressing over all.

4 LARGE, FIRM GREEN THAI PAPAYAS*

4 LARGE, FIRM TOMATOES

3 HEADS BOSTON LETTUCE

CAYENNE PEPPER TO TASTE

SERVES 12

SHRIMP AND LEMON GRASS SOUP

3 STALKS FRESH LEMON GRASS, SLICED THIN*

2 CUPS CANNED STRAW MUSHROOMS, WELL DRAINED

1½ POUNDS SHRIMP, SHELLED AND DEVEINED

2 TABLESPOONS NAM PLA (ORIENTAL FISH SAUCE)*

Bring 10 cups of water to a boil in a heavy saucepan over high heat. Add the lemon grass and the straw mushrooms. Immediately reduce the heat to medium and add the shrimp. Cook for 3 minutes. Stir in the Nam Pla and lime juice.

Remove the soup from the heat. Pour it into individual serving bowls and sprinkle each with scallions, coriander and red chili pepper. Lay one sprig of coriander in the center of each bowl and serve immediately.

¾ CUP FRESH LIME JUICE

½ CUP CHOPPED SCALLIONS

½ CUP CHOPPED FRESH CORIANDER (CILANTRO)

1 TABLESPOON MINCED FRESH RED CHILI PEPPER

12 CORIANDER SPRIGS

SERVES 12

STRING BEANS WITH FRESH GINGER

2 POUNDS FRESH STRING BEANS

2 TABLESPOONS CORN OIL

2 STALKS FRESH LEMON GRASS, FINELY CHOPPED*

2 TABLESPOONS MINCED FRESH GINGER ROOT

Wash the string beans and cut them into a julienne. Set aside.

Heat the oil in a wok over high heat. Lower the heat and sauté the lemon grass, ginger root, and red chili pepper until just slightly brown. Add the coconut milk and bring the mixture to a boil. Boil for 1 minute, then toss in the string beans. Add salt to taste and sauté until the beans are bright green. Serve immediately.

1 RED CHILI PEPPER, SEEDED, DEVEINED, AND FINELY CHOPPED

1 CUP FRESH COCONUT MILK

SALT TO TASTE

SERVES 12

POMELO SALAD

3 RIPE POMELOS (ORIENTAL CITRUS FRUIT)*

2 TABLESPOONS FRESH LEMON JUICE

3 TABLESPOONS NAM PLA (ORIENTAL FISH SAUCE)*

2 TABLESPOONS RED CHILI PEPPER PUREE

2 TABLESPOONS SUGAR

Peel the pomelos and scoop out their flesh, separating out the grains with your hands. Set aside.

In a food processor, using the metal blade, combine the lemon juice, Nam Pla, red chili pepper purée, and sugar. When they are well blended, stir in the coconut and coconut milk.

Place the basil leaves in small stacks. Tightly roll each stack and slice the rolls into thin sections. When all the rolls are sliced, toss to break them apart into shreds. Set aside.

Toss together the pomelo, roast pork, cooked shrimp, and the dressing. To serve, garnish with basil shreds.

3 TABLESPOONS TOASTED UNSWEETENED COCONUT

½ CUP COCONUT MILK

1 CUP FRESH BASIL LEAVES, WASHED AND DRIED

½ CUP DICED ROAST PORK

1 CUP DICED COOKED SHRIMP

SERVES 12

TARO AND CELERY ROOT CHIPS

Peel the taro root and slice it into paper-thin slices (as you would potatoes for potato chips). Set aside.

Peel the celery root and slice it into paper-thin slices. Toss the taro and celery root slices with the lemon juice and set aside.

Pour the oil into a deep fat fryer and heat it to 365° on a cooking thermometer. Place the slices, a few at a time, in the fry basket and cook them for about 1 minute, or until crisp and slightly brown.

Drain the chips on a paper towel and sprinkle them with salt to taste.

2 POUNDS TARO ROOT

2 POUNDS CELERY ROOT

2 TABLESPOONS FRESH LEMON JUICE

6 CUPS VEGETABLE OIL

SALT TO TASTE

SERVES 12

A trio of greens: Pomelo Salad, Seasoned Cucumbers, and String Beans with Fresh Ginger.

TAKAW

In a bowl, mix the tapioca flour, sugar, and water until smooth. Strain the mixture through a damp cheesecloth into a medium-sized saucepan. Cook over medium heat, stirring constantly, until thick and clear. Remove the pan from the heat and add the rose water.

Pour the flour mixture into small fluted-paper or foil muffin cups, filling each half full. Place the cups on a cookie sheet and refrigerate while preparing the next layer.

In a clean saucepan cook the rice flour and coconut milk over medium heat, stirring constantly, for 5 minutes, or until thick.

Remove the cups from the refrigerator and pour the coconut custard into each. Refrigerate for 1 hour, or until firm, then serve.

½ CUP TAPIOCA FLOUR

6 TABLESPOONS SUGAR

1⅓ CUPS WATER

1 TEASPOON ROSE WATER

2 TABLESPOONS RICE FLOUR

1 CUP COCONUT MILK

SERVES 12

STYLE
and
CONCEPTS

THE ONLY WAY TO HOST A PARTY IS IN YOUR OWN STYLE. VERY SIMPLY, YOUR STYLE IS YOUR attitude toward life; it is what will make your party unique. Preferences you have developed from everything you have seen, heard, tasted, felt, and learned should come together to help you plan an event that expresses who you are. The dictates of others do not decide the road to follow. Style is saying "No" as well as "Yes" and knowing the difference between the two. As professionals, we find that the hosts who are comfortable with their visions of what is to be accomplished lead us to the most exciting solutions.

Confidence is essential when you choose to be a host. Never forget that you are the master of ceremonies, you will set the tone and direct the event—sometimes quite literally, by playing the piano or leading games, and at other times simply by being the dominant force in the room. Your responses will dictate those of your guests; if you are harried, your guests will be uncomfortable. Your party should be an interlude, not an interruption—a time for you to shine.

Give yourself time to experiment before committing to any plan. Think about all the personal touches you'll want to make. Memories of these stylistic selections are the "favors" your guests will take away with them; they should clearly represent you, your company, or your charity.

Adventurous party concepts are limited only by your imagination.

Preparing the party location to express the theme.

If the style you have decided upon does not feel comfortable, reevaluate, but don't discard it until you're certain your discomfort is not just plain fear of developing yourself on a new level. If it's not too risky, try it. Be daring! Your guests will appreciate your adventurousness.

There are times, however, when your own sense of style has to take a backseat. In planning a child's party, for example, you should let the child make some of his own choices. It is a party for children, afterall, and often the child will know what's in style with his age group better than you do. Frequently, a child's vision can refresh yours.

At family gatherings your personal style can direct proceedings, but a stronger family style will probably prevail. Have fun delegating responsibility and bringing your taste to bear, and everyone will have a good time.

When you're entertaining important clients, or your boss or colleagues, the rule of thumb is to do what you do best. This is not the time to experiment with unknowns. The inherent style of your home and your natural graciousness will make a perfectly appropriate style statement. If you know that your business guests are in store for four or five nights of expense-account dining, plan an evening of elegant, at-home simplicity. Emphasize healthy, fresh foods, a simple tabletop, and an early end to the festivities. You will have given your guests what they can really appreciate—a night off.

The style of the corporate host must be a reflection of the stature of the corporation as well as an indication of the host's prominence within the company. The goals must be in keeping with the corporate hierarchy and history. Most frequently the goal is to allow guests to gather information about the corporation.

Since the name of the game in business entertaining is often "follow the leader," it is particularly rewarding to set a new style as a corporate host. Be courageous, forward-thinking, and bold in your approach. It is these very elements that put a company

Corporate entertaining is a studied understatement in which enjoyment does not interfere with business.

on the cutting edge. However, if your corporation is known for its conservative nature, take care to reflect its classic style in your plan.

All business hosting is business. Cocktail parties, ballroom dinners, new-product introductions, breakfast sales meetings—all are work and therefore never completely relaxed. But if the corporation organizes the event creatively, clients/guests will respond to their concerned approach.

A public event proclaims the style of the institution that hosts it. A fine arts guild will raise funds quite differently from a political candidate. Charity balls are the most extravagant means. The donor/guest support should be received with the same style in which it was given—glamour and elegance only spur a generous response.

Every party should have a theme, which is simply a creative way of expressing your goals. Consider an unusual theme, taking a concept out of its normal context. A luau is expected in July; but in snowy February a lifeless loft turned into a sandy beach,

The artwork in this public atrium inspires the party concept.

A party at the Temple of Dendur in The Metropolitan Museum of Art needs no embellishment, just illumination.

complete with orchids and palm trees, is a welcome surprise. Or imagine the possibilities of an elegant Thirties Tea Dance—polished, refined, and quiet, in gentle surroundings with proper service. A specific theme, such as "An Afternoon at the Circus," is simpler to manage than a general one, such as a costume ball, unless you narrow the requirements—asking guests to dress in a particular style or period, for instance. We created a "We Are Hot" party, complete with hot and spicy foods, in a firemen's museum to celebrate a company's successful sales report.

The most important choice you will make in determining a theme is whether the guests are expected to become "actors," by wearing costumes or playing games, or whether their presence is all that is needed to make the party complete. The theme, once chosen, should be carried out in the invitation, food, decor, music, favors, and, frequently, the style of dress. It should unfold with the polish of a well-written drama, yet be open to spontaneous improvisation. All parties are and should be fun.

Throw large parties only when you have an enormous storehouse of energy and time to plan every detail. Although opulent entertaining is intoxicating at any time, that long, long lull between Christmas and the advent of spring is the perfect time for a big bash. And you'll enjoy planning it at your leisure after the holiday rush.

With a solid sense of style and the imaginative development of a theme, your party will sparkle. We watch it happen every day.

ABOVE *Style is visual—accentuate what you own.*
TOP *A floating birthday cake.*

A Chinese Buffet by the Pool

GLAZED WALNUTS

RADISH FANS

SHRIMP BALLS WITH APRICOT SAUCE

SLICED LEMON CHICKEN

BEEF AND SNOW PEA SALAD

SWEET AND PUNGENT LOTUS ROOT

FIVE HEAPS

ASPARAGUS WITH RICE WINE VINAIGRETTE

SESAME NOODLES

GINGER ICE CREAM WITH FRESH LICHEES

When our hostess asked us to create a "casual" lunch for her summer weekend guests, we understood that casual to her meant something with panache and style. So we produced an informal but elegant Chinese meal, an idea inspired by her collection of Oriental pottery. A bench built around a tree trunk at the edge of her swimming pool became the buffet table. This special setting brought the crowd together and offered a break from the summer sun.

Since the afternoon was casual, no serving staff was needed. The food was prepared ahead in our commissary and served from the hostess's kitchen on her own dinnerware, using her serving pieces. We garnished and set out the buffet while the guests were on a tour of the property. When they returned, they were happy to dig in; most were even game enough to use chopsticks.

Ginger Ice Cream with Fresh Lichees is a wonderful finale for a Chinese buffet.

Glazed Walnuts

½ CUP COLD WATER

1 ½ TEASPOONS
    SUGAR

2 TEASPOONS
    MALTOSE*

¼ POUND WALNUT
    HALVES

½ CUP CORN OIL

SERVES 12

Combine the water, sugar, and maltose in a heavy saucepan and bring to a boil over medium-high heat. Stir to dissolve the sugars and boil for 1 minute. Add the nuts and swirl to coat them. Reduce the heat and cook for 7 minutes, or until only 2 tablespoons of liquid remain in the pan.

In another saucepan, using a candy thermometer, heat the oil to 275°. Scoop the nuts into the hot oil, being certain that they don't stick together. Fry them for 3 minutes, or until crispy and golden brown. Scoop the nuts out of the oil and separate them immediately on waxed paper laced over a wire rack to cool. When they are cool, blot the nuts with a paper towel.

Store uncovered at room temperature.

NOTE: INGREDIENTS MARKED WITH AN ASTERISK (*) CAN BE FOUND IN THE ORIENTAL SECTIONS OF MOST SUPERMARKETS, SPECIALTY STORES, AND ORIENTAL MARKETS.

Radish Fans

24 LARGE, OVAL-
    SHAPED,
    UNBLEMISHED RED
    RADISHES

2 TABLESPOONS
    LIGHT SOY SAUCE

2 TABLESPOONS
    RICE WINE
    VINEGAR*

1 TABLESPOON
    SUGAR

1 TABLESPOON
    SESAME OIL

SERVES 12

Wash the radishes and blot them dry. Trim the leaves off, leaving an attractive small sprig of leaf, if possible. Cut off the root end smoothly. Slice the radishes crosswise about ¹⁄₁₆-inch apart, being very careful not to slice through.

Place the sliced radishes into a large bowl of iced water to cover, and refrigerate for at least 3 hours. When the "fans" have opened, remove the radishes from the water and drain.

Combine the soy sauce, vinegar, sugar, and sesame oil. Whisk them until the sugar is dissolved.

Pour the dressing over the fans and marinate for 1 hour. Drain and serve.

SHRIMP BALLS
WITH APRICOT SAUCE

¾ POUND RAW
  SHRIMP, PEELED
  AND DEVEINED
¼ CUP MINCED
  WATER
  CHESTNUTS
2 TABLESPOONS
  MINCED
  SCALLIONS
1 TABLESPOON
  MINCED FRESH
  GARLIC
1 TEASPOON MINCED
  FRESH GINGER
  ROOT

In a food processor, using the metal blade, finely chop the raw shrimp. Add the minced water chestnuts, scallions, garlic, ginger root, and sesame oil.

Beat the egg whites until foamy and add to the shrimp, stirring in a fast circular motion with a wooden spoon or chopsticks. Combine the cornstarch and water and add to the shrimp. Stir in a circular motion until smooth and fluffy.

Grease your fingers and palm with oil and form the mixture into walnut-sized balls.

Heat the vegetable oil to 365°, measured on a cooking thermometer, in a deep saucepan. Deep fry the shrimp balls for about 3 minutes, or until crisp and golden. Remove them from the oil and drain on wire racks. Serve warm, with Apricot Sauce.

½ TEASPOON SESAME
  OIL
WHITES OF 2 LARGE
  EGGS
2 TABLESPOONS
  CORNSTARCH
2 TABLESPOONS
  COLD WATER
2 CUPS VEGETABLE
  OIL
APRICOT SAUCE

SERVES 12

APRICOT SAUCE

Combine the apricots, apricot nectar, sugar, vinegar, and ginger root in a medium saucepan over high heat. Bring to a boil. Lower the heat and simmer, stirring occasionally, for 30 minutes, or until the apricots are soft.

Dissolve the cornstarch in the water and add to the apricot mixture. Simmer for 2 minutes, or until incorporated. Remove the sauce from the heat and allow it to cool.

In a food processor, using the metal blade, process the apricot mixture until puréed. Serve at room temperature.

14 DRIED APRICOTS
2 CUPS APRICOT
  NECTAR
½ CUP SUGAR
½ CUP RICE WINE
  VINEGAR*
2 TABLESPOONS
  GRATED FRESH
  GINGER ROOT
1 TEASPOON
  CORNSTARCH
1 TABLESPOON COLD
  WATER

A simple braid of Chinese long beans makes an excellent garnish.

SLICED LEMON CHICKEN

3 POUNDS
  BONELESS
  CHICKEN BREASTS
4 CUPS FRESH
  CHICKEN STOCK
  (SEE PAGE 37)
1 ½-INCH-LONG PIECE
  OF PEELED
  GINGER ROOT
1 TEASPOON GRATED
  FRESH LEMON
  RIND
¼ CUP FRESH LEMON
  JUICE
3 TABLESPOONS
  SUGAR
3½ TABLESPOONS
  CORNSTARCH

Place the chicken breasts in a shallow pan and cover them with the Chicken Stock. Crush the ginger root with the side of a cleaver or knife and add to the chicken in the pan. Bring the liquid to a simmer over medium heat and poach the chicken for 10 minutes, or until just done. Remove the chicken from the liquid and set it aside to cool.

Strain the broth through a fine sieve and add the lemon rind, lemon juice, and sugar. Stir to blend. Place the liquid in a saucepan over medium heat. Remove ½ cup of the liquid, mix the cornstarch into it, and then briskly whisk the cornstarch mixture into the saucepan. Add salt and pepper to taste. Lower the heat and continue cooking for about 3 minutes, or until the sauce is thick.

Place the snow peas in rapidly boiling water for about 30 seconds, or until brightly colored and still crisp. Immediately remove them to iced water. When they are cool, drain them and pat dry.

Slice the chicken, scallions, and celery on the diagonal.

Lay the slices of chicken on a serving plate in a curving fan shape. Nestle the straw mushrooms at the bottom of the curve. Top the chicken with a layer of celery, then scallions. Arrange the snow peas around the outer edge of the chicken and drizzle the entire plate with sauce. Sprinkle the chopped coriander and sesame seeds over all.

SALT AND PEPPER
  TO TASTE
½ POUND SNOW PEAS
2 BUNCHES
  SCALLIONS
6 STALKS CELERY
¾ CUP CANNED
  STRAW
  MUSHROOMS,
  WELL DRAINED*
¼ CUP CHOPPED
  FRESH CORIANDER
  (CILANTRO)
1 TABLESPOON
  TOASTED SESAME
  SEEDS

SERVES 12

The piquant flavor of Sweet and Pungent Lotus Root offsets the heartiness of a Beef and Snow Pea Salad.

BEEF AND SNOW PEA SALAD

3 POUNDS SIRLOIN TIPS

2 CUPS SOY SAUCE

¼ CUP SHERRY

3½ TABLESPOONS GRATED GINGER ROOT

1 TABLESPOON MINCED FRESH GARLIC

3 TABLESPOONS SUGAR

¾ POUND SNOW PEAS, TRIMMED

¾ CUP RICE WINE VINEGAR*

2 TABLESPOONS SESAME OIL

WHITE PEPPER TO TASTE

1 TABLESPOON PEANUT OIL

¾ CUP SLICED WATER CHESTNUTS

2 PACKAGES ENOKI MUSHROOMS, TRIMMED*

SERVES 12

Marinate the beef in 1 cup of the soy sauce, the sherry wine, 2½ tablespoons of the ginger root, the garlic, and 1 teaspoon of the sugar.

Place the snow peas in rapidly boiling water for about 30 seconds, or until brightly colored but still crisp. Immediately remove them to ice water. When they are cool, drain and pat dry. Set aside.

Mix the remaining soy sauce, ginger root, and sugar with the vinegar, sesame oil, and white pepper. Whisk to combine.

Heat the peanut oil in a heavy sauté pan. Remove the beef from the marinade and sauté it quickly for 4 minutes, or until medium rare. Drain it well on a paper towel. Slice into bite-sized pieces and blend with the soy vinaigrette. Toss in the water chestnuts.

Arrange the snow peas around the edge of a serving platter. Place the beef and water chestnuts on top, with enoki mushrooms in a nest in the center of the beef.

Serve at room temperature.

SWEET AND PUNGENT LOTUS ROOT

2 POUNDS LOTUS
  ROOT (FRESH OR
  CANNED)*
¼ CUP PEANUT OIL
½ TEASPOON
  TABASCO SAUCE
2 TABLESPOONS
  SUGAR
¼ CUP RICE WINE
  VINEGAR*
¼ CUP SOY SAUCE
½ TEASPOON SESAME
  OIL

SERVES 12

Peel the lotus root. Cut it lengthwise in half; then slice it very thin. Soak the slices for 10 minutes in 8 cups of iced water. Drain and pat them dry.

Bring 6 cups of water to a boil. Pour it over the lotus root and let stand 2 minutes. Drain. Cool the slices under cold running water and drain again. Pat them dry.

Heat the oil in a heavy sauté pan over medium heat. Quickly stir in the Tabasco sauce, remove the mixture from the heat, and stir in the sugar, vinegar, soy sauce, and sesame oil. Whisk to combine.

Place the lotus root in a bowl and pour in the warm dressing. Toss to coat. Refrigerate, covered, for 20 minutes or until just chilled.

FIVE HEAPS

½ POUND LONG, THIN
  CHINESE EGG
  NOODLES
¼ CUP PLUS 2
  TEASPOONS
  SAFFLOWER OIL
¼ CUP TOASTED
  SESAME SEEDS
¼ CUP SESAME
  PASTE
2 TABLESPOONS
  COLD WATER
2 TABLESPOONS
  LIGHT SOY SAUCE
4 TEASPOONS RICE
  WINE VINEGAR*
1 TABLESPOON
  SUGAR
ROASTED SZECHUAN
  PEPPER TO TASTE*
1 TEASPOON CHILI
  OIL

SALT TO TASTE
2 CUPS FRESH BEAN
  SPROUTS
2 CUPS SNOW PEAS
  (OR SUGAR SNAP
  PEAS)
2 CUPS SHREDDED
  CARROTS
2 CUPS SHREDDED
  RADISHES
2 CUPS SLIVERED
  BLACK FOREST
  HAM (OR COOKED
  CHICKEN BREAST)
½ CUP COARSELY
  CHOPPED FRESH
  CORIANDER
  (CILANTRO)

SERVES 12

Reserve 2 teaspoons of the sesame seeds and add the remainder to the bowl of a food processor fitted with a metal blade. Process until coarsely ground. Add ¼ cup of the safflower oil, the sesame paste, water, soy sauce, vinegar, sugar, Szechuan pepper, chili oil, and salt and process until well blended. Remove the mixture from the processor bowl and let it stand at room temperature for at least 4 hours to develop the flavors.

Cook the noodles according to package directions. Drain them well and toss them with 2 teaspoons of the safflower oil.

Blanch the bean sprouts for 20 seconds in rapidly boiling water. Drain them, and rinse under cold running water. Drain again, and pat them dry.

Blanch the snow peas in rapidly boiling water for 30 seconds until tender-crisp. Drain, chill them under cold water, and pat them dry.

Pour the sauce over the noodles, mixing well to coat the strands. Mound the noodles in the center of a serving platter, then ring the noodles with the bean sprouts, snow peas, carrots, radishes, and ham (these represent the Five Heaps), alternating them for the most colorful effect. Sprinkle the reserved sesame seeds and chopped coriander on top and serve immediately.

ASPARAGUS WITH RICE WINE VINAIGRETTE

½ CUP SAFFLOWER
  OIL
¾ CUP LIGHT SOY
  SAUCE
1 CUP RICE WINE
  VINEGAR*
2 CLOVES GARLIC,
  MASHED

Whisk together the oil, soy sauce, and vinegar. Add the garlic, ginger root, shallot, and pepper. Stir to combine and set aside for 1 hour.

Trim the asparagus to make uniform, slender stalks.

In rapidly boiling salted water, blanch the asparagus for 2 minutes, or until bright green. Remove it to iced water. When chilled, drain and pat it dry.

Arrange the asparagus on a serving platter. Strain the garlic, shallot, and ginger from the vinaigrette. Whisk the vinaigrette and pour it over the asparagus. Serve immediately.

1 2-INCH-PIECE
  FRESH GINGER
  ROOT, PEELED
  AND CRUSHED
1 SHALLOT, HALVED
PINCH PEPPER
60 STALKS
  ASPARAGUS

SERVES 12

Asparagus is given an Oriental accent with rice wine vinaigrette.

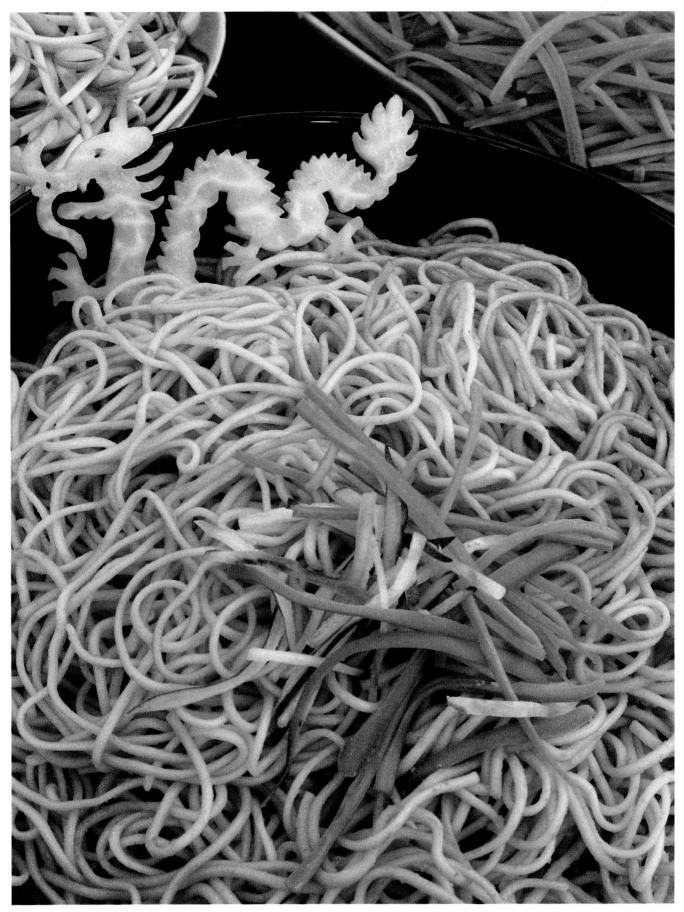

Dragons cut from Chinese white radish enliven Sesame Noodles surrounded by the Five Heaps.

SESAME NOODLES

3 TABLESPOONS
TOASTED SESAME
SEEDS

¾ CUP SMOOTH
PEANUT BUTTER

1 TABLESPOON COLD
WATER

1½ TABLESPOONS
RICE WINE
VINEGAR*

2¼ TEASPOONS
SUGAR

3 TABLESPOONS
LIGHT SOY SAUCE

¼ TEASPOON
GROUND
SZECHUAN
PEPPER*

SALT TO TASTE

¼ TEASPOON CHILI
OIL

1½ POUNDS CHINESE
EGG NOODLES

2 TABLESPOONS
SESAME OIL

¾ POUND BEAN
SPROUTS

¾ POUND CHINESE
ROASTED PORK*

3 MEDIUM
CUCUMBERS

2 BUNCHES
RADISHES

SERVES 12

Reserve 1 teaspoon of the sesame seeds. Place the remaining sesame seeds in a food processor bowl. Using the metal blade, process them until finely ground. Add the peanut butter, water, vinegar, sugar, soy sauce, ground Szechuan pepper, and salt to taste. Process to blend, then mix in the chili oil. Remove the sauce from the processor bowl. Cover and refrigerate it at least 2 hours.

Cook the noodles according to the package directions. Drain them and toss in the sesame oil. Cover and refrigerate.

Place the bean sprouts in rapidly boiling water for about 20 seconds, or until just blanched. Immediately remove them to iced water. When they are cool, drain them and pat dry.

Shred the roasted pork.

Peel, seed, and julienne the cucumbers. Trim and julienne the radishes.

Toss the noodles in the sesame sauce and garnish with shredded pork, bean sprouts, and julienned vegetables.

GINGER ICE CREAM
WITH FRESH LICHEES

1 CUP SUGAR

¾ CUP COLD WATER

6 LARGE EGG YOLKS

½ CUP SYRUP FROM
COMMERCIALLY
PREPARED
PRESERVED
GINGER

½ TEASPOON GRATED
FRESH GINGER
ROOT

1 CUP FINELY
CHOPPED CANDIED
GINGER

1 TEASPOON FRESH
LIME JUICE

4 CUPS HEAVY
CREAM, WHIPPED

FRESH LICHEES*

SERVES 12

In a heavy saucepan over high heat, bring the sugar and water to a boil. Boil, stirring frequently, until a candy thermometer inserted in the mixture registers 215°. Allow it to cool slightly.

With an electric mixer, beat the egg yolks until they are thick and pale yellow. Slowly pour in the cooled sugar syrup, beating as you pour. When well combined, add the ginger syrup, gingers, and lime juice.

Fold in the whipped cream.

Pour the mixture into an ice cream maker and freeze according to the manufacturer's directions. Serve with fresh lichees.

A Special Corporate Fourth of July

AVOCADO AND GRAPEFRUIT SALAD

SLICED SUGARED STEAK

PICKLED BLACK-EYED PEAS

RED BLISS POTATOES WITH
CRACKED MUSTARD

CORN FRITTERS WITH GREEN
TOMATO CHUTNEY

TASSIES

For the much-celebrated hundredth birthday of the Statue of Liberty, our corporate host wanted to create a memorable weekend for their employees and clients. Knowing of their business philosophy and financial confidence in America, we decided that the theme had to be red, white, and blue. We transformed a boat into a gigantic floating birthday cake, topped with enormous cardboard candles. The interior was filled with American flags and tricolor balloons and the exterior was "iced" with red, white, and blue star-shaped lights and banners. A huge replica of the American flag was created by stacking red, white, and blue box dinners on a covered deck.

Throughout the weekend, different groups were treated to rides on the "birthday cake". As they cruised down the river to the foot of Lady Liberty, strains of "God Bless America" and "Happy Birthday" filled the air, while the guests enjoyed delicious American cuisine. It was a gala tribute to the solidarity of the corporation, its delight in its guests, and a strong belief in America.

Box dinners arranged on a low buffet form a graphic presentation of the American Flag.

Specially created china brings the Fourth of July theme to the tabletop.

Avocado and Grapefruit Salad

4 RIPE AVOCADOS
2 TEASPOONS FRESH
  LEMON JUICE
2 BUNCHES
  WATERCRESS,
  TRIMMED
4 PINK GRAPEFRUITS,
  SECTIONED

Peel and slice the avocados. Sprinkle them with 1 teaspoon of the lemon juice to prevent discoloring.

Place equal portions of watercress on each of 12 salad plates. Alternate slices of avocado and grapefruit sections on top of the watercress. Whisk together the mayonnaise, honey, remaining lemon juice, onion juice, and paprika and pour the dressing over the salad. Serve immediately.

1 CUP MAYONNAISE
¼ CUP HONEY
1 TEASPOON ONION
  JUICE
PINCH HUNGARIAN
  PAPRIKA

SERVES 12

Sliced Sugared Steak

Have the butcher cut the steaks about 2½ inches thick, with ample surrounding fat and the chuck end left on.

Work ¾ cup of the sugar into both sides of the steaks with the heel of your hand until they have absorbed all the sugar and the meat shows red again. Use wooden skewers to hold the tails of the steaks in place. Sear the steaks on a hot grill (or griddle) for 5 minutes per side to seal. Cook them for an additional 10 minutes, turning frequently, for a medium-rare steak.

Do not salt the steaks while cooking. Put the butter, salt, and pepper on a platter, place the steaks on top of the butter, and cut them on the bias. Serve immediately or chill and serve later at room temperature.

2 6-POUND
  PORTERHOUSE
  STEAKS
3 CUPS SUGAR
¼ POUND SALTED
  BUTTER
SALT AND PEPPER
  TO TASTE

SERVES 12

Pickled Black-eyed Peas

Wash the peas. Cover them with cold water and let them soak overnight.

Pour the peas into a heavy saucepan, add water to cover, and bring them to a boil over medium heat. Add 4 slices of onion, 1 clove of garlic, and the bay leaves. Lower the heat and cook for approximately 1 hour, or until the peas are tender. Drain off the liquid.

Whisk together the vinegar, oil, salt and pepper. Taste, and adjust the seasonings. Pour the vinaigrette over the drained peas. Cover and refrigerate for at least 12 hours. Remove the garlic and bay leaves before serving.

¾ POUND BLACK-
  EYED PEAS
1 LARGE ONION,
  SLICED
2 CLOVES FRESH
  GARLIC, HALVED
3 BAY LEAVES
⅔ CUP CIDER
  VINEGAR
1¼ CUPS CORN OIL
SALT AND PEPPER
  TO TASTE

SERVES 12

RED BLISS POTATOES WITH CRACKED MUSTARD

3 POUNDS SMALL
RED BLISS
POTATOES,
COOKED AND
QUARTERED
¾ CUP CHOPPED
CELERY
1 CUP CHOPPED
SCALLIONS
¾ CUP DICED GREEN
PEPPERS

Combine the potatoes, celery, scallions, green peppers, and parsley. Whisk together the vinegar, oil, and mustard. When well blended, add the salt and pepper to taste. Pour the vinaigrette over the vegetables and gently toss to combine. Serve at room temperature.

2 TABLESPOONS
MINCED FRESH
ITALIAN PARSLEY
2 TABLESPOONS RED
WINE VINEGAR
½ CUP OLIVE OIL
¼ CUP CRACKED
MUSTARD
SALT AND PEPPER
TO TASTE

SERVES 12

CORN FRITTERS WITH GREEN TOMATO CHUTNEY

2 LARGE EGGS
½ CUP CANNED
CREAMED CORN
½ CUP CANNED
WHITE-KERNEL
CORN
2 TABLESPOONS
YELLOW CORN
MEAL
¼ CUP ALL-PURPOSE
FLOUR
1 TEASPOON BAKING
POWDER

Beat the eggs and add the creamed corn and corn kernels. Stir in the corn meal, flour, baking powder, nutmeg, and salt and pepper to taste. When well blended, stir in the melted butter.

Heat the oil in a heavy sauté pan over medium heat. When it is hot, lower the heat and drop the batter in by the tablespoonful to make fritters. Fry the fritters for about 1 minute, or until light brown, then turn them and brown the other side. Serve them with Green Tomato Chutney.

PINCH GROUND
NUTMEG
1 TEASPOON SALT
PINCH PEPPER
2 TABLESPOONS
MELTED SALTED
BUTTER
½ CUP CORN OIL
GREEN TOMATO
CHUTNEY

SERVES 12

GREEN TOMATO CHUTNEY

2 TABLESPOONS
COARSE SALT
3 CUPS SLICED
GREEN TOMATOES
⅓ CUP CIDER
VINEGAR
½ CUP HONEY
2 TABLESPOONS
MINCED FRESH
GARLIC
⅓ CUP CURRANTS

Sprinkle the salt over the tomatoes and let them stand overnight. Drain and place the tomatoes in a heavy saucepan with the remaining ingredients. Bring to a boil over medium heat. Lower the heat and let the chutney simmer for about 2 hours, or until thickened, stirring often. Serve at room temperature.

¼ CUP FINELY
CHOPPED CANDIED
GINGER
1 CUP PEELED,
CORED, AND
CHOPPED GREEN
APPLE
2 CUPS CHOPPED
ONION
⅓ CUP CHOPPED
FRESH MINT

TASSIES

Blend the cup of butter, cream cheese, and flour in a food processor, using the metal blade. Chill for 1 hour. Form the pastry into 12 small balls and press each down into a miniature muffin cup to form a tiny tart shell. Using a fork, prick each shell on the bottom and sides. Set them aside.

Preheat the oven to 375°.

Fill each shell with pastry weights, dried beans, or rice, and bake shells for 10 minutes or until light brown. Cool them in the pans, and then remove the weights, beans, or rice, and fill.

1 CUP UNSALTED BUTTER
1 8-OUNCE PACKAGE CREAM CHEESE
2 CUPS ALL-PURPOSE FLOUR
LEMON CHEESE FILLING
STRAWBERRY FILLING
BLUEBERRY FILLING

SERVES 12

TOP *A barbershop quartet greets guests.*
ABOVE *New York Harbor all aglow in celebration.*

LEMON CHEESE FILLING

Beat the eggs in the top half of a double boiler over boiling water until they are thick and fluffy. Continue beating them while you add the sugar, lemon juice, and rind. Cook the mixture over hot water until it is smooth and thick. Allow it to cool.

Beat the cream cheese until it is smooth and gradually blend the lemon custard into it. Fill the baked mini-pastry shells and garnish them with the sweetened whipped cream, if desired.

3 LARGE EGGS
¾ CUP SUGAR
½ CUP FRESH LEMON JUICE
2 TEASPOONS GRATED FRESH LEMON RIND
1 8-OUNCE PACKAGE CREAM CHEESE
1 CUP SWEETENED WHIPPED CREAM (OPTIONAL)

STRAWBERRY FILLING

2 CUPS CRUSHED FRESH STRAWBERRIES
4 CUPS SUGAR
1 ½ TEASPOONS FRESH LEMON JUICE

Mix the strawberries, sugar, and lemon juice together and let stand. Meanwhile mix the pectin and water and boil for 1 minute. Add the strawberry mixture and allow it to cool. Fill the baked mini-pastry shells and garnish them with the sweetened whipped cream, if desired.

1 BOX COMMERCIAL PECTIN
1 CUP BOILING WATER
1 CUP SWEETENED WHIPPED CREAM (OPTIONAL)

BLUEBERRY FILLING

1 3-OUNCE PACKAGE CREAM CHEESE
1 CUP SUGAR
¼ CUP HEAVY CREAM, WHIPPED
1 15-OUNCE CAN BLUEBERRIES
2 TABLESPOONS ALL PURPOSE FLOUR

Beat the cream cheese, ⅜ cup of the sugar, and the heavy cream together until fluffy. Cover and refrigerate.

Reserve one quarter of the blueberry juice in the can and put the remainder of the contents in a heavy saucepan over low heat.

Mix the dry ingredients together and add them to the fruit. Mix well, but gently. Add the lemon juice and the butter. Cook over medium heat, stirring constantly, until the mixture has thickened. Allow it to cool.

Spread the cheese mixture over the bottom of the baked mini-pastry shells, then fill them with the blueberry filling. Reserve enough of the cheese mixture to put a small dollop on top of each tart.

¼ TEASPOON GROUND NUTMEG
1 TABLESPOON FRESH LEMON JUICE
1 TABLESPOON UNSALTED BUTTER

The Opening of the Siena Exhibition

CHICKEN ROULADE

PUMPKIN-STUFFED MUSHROOMS

POLENTA CANAPES

SHRIMP WITH ROASTED PEPPER SAUCE

GRAVLAX

GORGONZOLA AND PIGNOLI CANAPES

STUFFED FOCACCIA WITH ROSEMARY

TORTELLINI WITH PEAS

SAVOIARDI

STRUFOLI

PANFORTE DI SIENA

TORRONE

PANETTONE

STIACCIATA

Sponsored by an Italian corporation, the opening of an exhibit of Renaissance paintings from Siena was celebrated early in the Christmas season in The Medieval Sculpture Hall of New York's Metropolitan Museum of Art. The Museum's magnificent Christmas tree, resplendent with Italian Baroque figures, was the centerpiece, surrounded by tables piled high with foods of Tuscany. Highlights were the pungent holiday desserts and beautifully arranged towers of luscious fruit.

The Medieval Sculpture Hall at The Metropolitan Museum of Art at Christmas season.

Chicken Roulade and Tortellini with Peas.

CHICKEN ROULADE

1 WHOLE BONELESS CHICKEN BREAST

1½ TABLESPOONS SUN-DRIED TOMATOES, PACKED IN OIL

1 TABLESPOON FRESH PUREED BASIL

2 OUNCES PROSCIUTTO

WHITE PEPPER TO TASTE

SERVES 12

Slice into the chicken breast, opening it like a book, but do not cut completely through. Lay the chicken between 2 sheets of waxed paper and pound until very thin.

Julienne the sun-dried tomatoes and set aside.

Rub the chicken with the basil purée and season it with white pepper. Spread on a single layer of prosciutto, leaving a ½-inch edge of chicken uncovered, and place a line of sun-dried tomatoes near this edge. Tightly roll the chicken, starting from the end with the tomatoes.

Wrap the roulade in clear food wrap, then in aluminum foil, twisting the ends tightly to secure it. Poach it in boiling water for 12 minutes. Remove it from the water and let it rest for at least 10 minutes before unwrapping the foil. Slice it on the bias in ¾-inch sections and serve either warm or at room temperature.

NOTE: QUANTITIES FOR APPETIZERS ARE BASED ON ONE SERVING PER PERSON BUT CAN BE DOUBLED.

PUMPKIN-STUFFED MUSHROOMS

½ POUND MEDIUM MUSHROOMS

2 TABLESPOONS UNSALTED BUTTER

1 TEASPOON MINCED FRESH GARLIC

¼ TEASPOON GROUND DRIED THYME

¼ TEASPOON GROUND DRIED ROSEMARY

¼ CUP PUREED SWEET POTATO (CANNED OR FRESH)

1 CUP PUMPKIN PUREE, WELL-DRAINED (CANNED OR FRESH)

2 TABLESPOONS GRATED PARMESAN CHEESE

SALT AND PEPPER TO TASTE

SERVES 12

Preheat the oven to 350°.

Brush the mushrooms but do not wash them. Remove the stems and reserve them for another use.

Melt the butter in a small sauté pan over medium heat. Lower the heat and sauté the garlic, thyme, and rosemary for about 3 minutes, or until the garlic is soft but not brown.

Mix in the sweet potato, pumpkin, 1 tablespoon of the Parmesan cheese, and salt and pepper to taste. When well blended, stuff each mushroom cap with the mixture. Sprinkle the remaining Parmesan on top of each and broil for about 2 minutes, or until the mushrooms are slightly cooked and the stuffing is hot. Serve warm.

POLENTA CANAPES

¼ CUP UNCOOKED INSTANT POLENTA

24 MEDIUM BUTTON MUSHROOMS

½ OUNCE DRIED PORCINI MUSHROOMS

1 TABLESPOON OLIVE OIL

½ TABLESPOON MINCED FRESH SHALLOTS

½ TEASPOON MINCED FRESH GARLIC

1 TEASPOON TOMATO PASTE

SALT AND PEPPER TO TASTE

1 TABLESPOON MELTED SALTED BUTTER

1 ROASTED RED PEPPER

24 TINY FRESH BASIL LEAVES

SERVES 12

Make the polenta according to the package directions. Spread it out ¼-inch thick on a buttered sheet pan. Cover and chill for at least 4 hours.

Preheat the oven to 500°.

Clean and stem the button mushrooms. Reserve the stems for another use.

Place the porcini mushrooms in hot water to cover. When they are reconstituted, drain well and chop fine.

Heat the olive oil in a small sauté pan over medium heat. Stir in the porcini, shallots, and garlic and cook for about 3 minutes, or until soft. Add the tomato paste and salt and pepper to taste and stir until well combined. Stuff the button mushrooms with the mixture. Brush them with the melted butter and bake them for 3 minutes.

Cut the chilled polenta into 1½-inch squares. Place a cooked mushroom in the center and a snip of Roasted Red Pepper in the corner. Garnish with a basil leaf tucked under each mushroom. Serve immediately.

ROASTED RED PEPPER

1 RED PEPPER

Stick a long fork with a heat-proof handle into the stem end of the red pepper and hold it as close as possible to a high flame. Turn frequently, until the pepper is charred and the skin has puffed away from the flesh. Immediately place the hot pepper into a paper or plastic bag and seal it tightly. Allow the pepper to set for 10 minutes, then remove it from the bag and gently pull off the charred skin. Stem and seed the pepper, but do not wash it. Cut it into a julienne.

For long storage, immerse the strips in olive oil, cover, and refrigerate.

SHRIMP WITH ROASTED PEPPER SAUCE

1 LARGE TOMATO

6 CLOVES GARLIC, UNPEELED

½ CUP OLIVE OIL

2 TABLESPOONS SLIVERED ALMONDS

1 ROASTED RED PEPPER (SEE PAGE 77)

¼ CUP RED WINE VINEGAR

PINCH RED PEPPER FLAKES

SALT AND PEPPER TO TASTE

1 POUND SHRIMP COOKED, SHELLED, AND DEVEINED

SERVES 12

Preheat the oven to 350°

Place the tomato and garlic cloves on a baking sheet and roast them for 30 minutes, or until soft. When they are cool, peel and seed the tomato and peel the garlic.

Heat the olive oil in a small sauté pan over medium heat. Add the almonds and sauté for 3 minutes, or until the almonds begin to turn light gold.

Place the tomato, garlic, and roasted pepper in a food processor fitted with a metal blade. Turn the motor on and gradually add the oil and almonds. While the motor is still running, add the vinegar, red pepper flakes, and salt and pepper to taste. Pour the sauce over the shrimp, and stir to combine. Cover and refrigerate for at least 6 hours. Serve cold.

Sliced Gravlax.

GRAVLAX

4 POUNDS FRESH SALMON FILLET

⅓ CUP LEMON-FLAVORED VODKA

½ CUP SUGAR

½ CUP COARSE SALT

3 TABLESPOONS COARSELY GROUND PEPPER

1 BUNCH DILL SPRIGS

1 BUNCH FRESH CHIVES

SERVES 12

Lay the salmon fillet in a glass baking dish. Pour the vodka over the salmon, turning it as necessary to coat.

Mix the sugar, salt, and pepper and gently rub the mixture into the salmon. Lay the dill and chives on top of the salmon and wrap the entire fillet in cheesecloth.

Wrap the dish in aluminum foil and seal it well. Place a heavy weight on top so that it rests on the wrapped fillet. Refrigerate for 3 days. Open the foil, turn, and baste the salmon every 12 hours, making certain that you rewrap it tightly and re-weight it carefully after each basting.

When you are ready to serve, remove the weight and unwrap the fish. Gently wipe off all marinade and herbs. To serve, slice on the bias.

GORGONZOLA AND PIGNOLI CANAPES

¼ CUP SALTED BUTTER
⅔ CUP GORGONZOLA CHEESE
1 TABLESPOON UNTOASTED PIGNOLI NUTS
PINCH PEPPER

4 LARGE BASIL LEAVES
12 BAKED MINI-TART SHELLS (SEE PAGE 29)
1¼ TABLESPOONS TOASTED PIGNOLI NUTS

SERVES 12

Blend the butter, cheese, and untoasted pignoli nuts in a food processor, using the metal blade. Add pepper to taste (the mixture should have a bite). Blend until it is smooth enough to pipe through a star-shaped tip on a pastry bag.

Cut the basil leaves into a fine chiffonade.

Pipe the cheese mixture into the baked mini-tart shells. Garnish with the toasted pignoli nuts and basil chiffonade.

STUFFED FOCACCIA WITH ROSEMARY

2 PACKETS ACTIVE DRY YEAST
1 CUP WARM WATER
3¼ CUPS ALL-PURPOSE FLOUR
1 TEASPOON SALT
⅔ CUP OLIVE OIL
1¼ CUPS CHOPPED FRESH ROSEMARY
½ CUP SUN-DRIED TOMATOES, PACKED IN OIL
6 SPRIGS FRESH BASIL, TRIMMED OF WOODY STEMS
½ POUND BUCHERON CHEESE
½ POUND CREAM CHEESE

SERVES 12

Dissolve the yeast in the warm water. Combine the flour, salt, and ⅓ cup of the olive oil. Stir in the yeast and water. When well combined, turn the dough out onto a floured surface and knead it into a small ball. (You may also knead it in an electric mixer or food processor.) Place the dough in a large bowl that has been coated generously with some of the olive oil. Cover it with a dry towel and place it in a warm, draft-free spot for 1 hour, or until double in volume.

When the dough has doubled, oil a 9 x 12-inch baking sheet and stretch the dough to fit in it. Cover it with a dry towel and let it rise for 30 minutes.

Preheat the oven to 400°.

Using your finger tips, make indentations in the top of the dough. Drizzle it with the remaining olive oil and sprinkle it evenly with the rosemary. Bake the focaccia for 20 to 25 minutes, or until golden. Set the bread aside to cool.

In a food processor, using a metal blade, chop the sun-dried tomatoes and basil. Add the Bucheron and cream cheese and mix until well blended.

Using a serrated knife, split the focaccia evenly as you would a sandwich roll. Spread the bottom half with the cheese mixture and cover it with the top half. Cut the focaccia into 1½-inch squares and serve it at room temperature.

TORTELLINI WITH PEAS

2 CUPS FROZEN PETIT PEAS

¼ CUP SALTED BUTTER

1 CUP FINELY CHOPPED ONION

1 EGG YOLK

1½ TABLESPOONS DIJON MUSTARD

3 TABLESPOONS BALSAMIC VINEGAR

1 CUP OLIVE OIL

SALT AND PEPPER TO TASTE

4 POUNDS CHEESE TORTELLINI

1 CUP CHOPPED FRESH ITALIAN PARSLEY

¾ CUP GRATED PARMESAN CHEESE

SERVES 12

Place the frozen peas in a colander under running tepid water. When they are thawed, set them aside to drain well.

Melt the butter in a medium sauté pan over low heat. Add the onion and sauté for about 10 minutes, or until brown. Set aside.

In a food processor, using the metal blade, combine the egg yolk, mustard, and vinegar. Slowly pour in the olive oil, with the motor running, and blend until thick. Add the onion and salt and pepper to taste. Set aside.

In rapidly boiling salted water, cook the tortellini according to the package directions. Drain well and toss with the dressing, peas, parsley, and Parmesan cheese. Serve immediately, or chill and serve at room temperature.

Assorted Tuscan desserts.

SAVOIARDI

Preheat the oven to 375°.

Beat the egg yolks and sugar until frothy and pale yellow. Add the flour and beat until smooth. Add the vanilla.

Beat the egg whites until they hold a peak. Fold them into the yolk mixture, mixing until no white streaks remain.

Butter and flour a 9 x 12-inch cookie sheet. Pour the batter by the tablespoonful onto the sheet, forming 3-inch fingers. Let them stand for 10 minutes. Bake for 10 minutes, or until the edges are just golden. When the savoiardi are cool, sift an ample amount of confectioners' sugar on top of each.

3 LARGE EGGS, SEPARATED
½ CUP SUGAR
½ CUP ALL-PURPOSE FLOUR
½ TEASPOON VANILLA EXTRACT
½ CUP CONFECTIONERS' SUGAR

SERVES 12

STRUFOLI

5 CUPS ALL-PURPOSE FLOUR
½ CUP UNSALTED BUTTER, SOFTENED
7 WHOLE LARGE EGGS
3 LARGE EGG YOLKS
1 TABLESPOON SUGAR

On a pastry board, form a mound with the flour making a well in the center. Place the butter, eggs, egg yolks, sugar, and lemon rind in the well. Using your hands, gently knead the ingredients together to form a pliant dough. Taking a handful at a time, form the dough into ropelike lengths about ½-inch thick. Cut each rope into ½-inch pieces, and roll them into marble-sized balls.

In a deep-fat fryer, heat the oil to 350°, measured on a cooking thermometer. Drop the balls, a few at a time, into the hot oil. Fry them for 2 minutes, or until golden. Drain them on paper towels. Pile them in a mound on a lightly greased serving dish.

In a small saucepan over low heat, melt the honey. Pour it over the mound of balls on the serving platter and sprinkle with colored confectionery sprinkles.

1 TEASPOON GRATED FRESH LEMON RIND
4 CUPS VEGETABLE OIL
3 CUPS HONEY
5 TABLESPOONS MULTICOLORED CONFECTIONERY SPRINKLES

SERVES 12

PANFORTE DI SIENA

¼ POUND HALVED HAZELNUTS
¼ POUND BLANCHED SLIVERED ALMONDS
1 CUP FINELY CHOPPED CANDIED ORANGE PEEL
½ CUP FINELY CHOPPED CANDIED CITRON PEEL
1 CUP FINELY CHOPPED CANDIED LEMON PEEL

Preheat the oven to 300°.

Line the sides and bottom of a 9-inch spring-form pan with buttered parchment paper (baking paper). Set aside.

Combine the nuts, citrus peels, flour, cocoa powder, and spices. Set aside.

In a small saucepan, over medium heat, melt the sugar into the honey, stirring constantly. When a candy thermometer registers 235°, remove the mixture from the heat and immediately stir it into the nut-fruit mixture until well blended.

Pour the batter into the prepared pan and spread it to coat evenly. Bake for 30 minutes. Remove from the heat and cool on a wire rack. When cool, remove the spring-form and generously sift the confectioners' sugar on top.

½ CUP CAKE FLOUR
½ CUP COCOA POWDER
1 TEASPOON GROUND CINNAMON
½ TEASPOON GROUND ALLSPICE
½ CUP SUGAR
1 CUP CLOVER HONEY
¼ CUP CONFECTIONERS' SUGAR

SERVES 12

TORRONE

8 SHEETS OSTIA
(UNLEAVENED WAFER
AVAILABLE IN ITALIAN
GOURMET SHOPS)
1 CUP CLOVER
HONEY
2 LARGE EGG WHITES
1 CUP SUGAR
¼ CUP COLD WATER
1 POUND BLANCHED
SLIVERED
ALMONDS

½ POUND TOASTED
HAZELNUTS
1½ TEASPOONS
FINELY DICED
CANDIED CITRON
1 TEASPOON GRATED
FRESH ORANGE
RIND

SERVES 12

Line two 4 x 8-inch pans with the Ostia.

In the top half of a double boiler, over boiling water, cook the honey for 1 hour, or until caramelized, stirring often. Remove from the heat.

Beat the egg whites until stiff. Gradually whip them into the caramelized honey until light and fluffy.

In a small saucepan, over high heat, boil the sugar and water for 15 minutes, or until caramelized. Slowly whip it into the honey mixture in the top half of the double boiler. Continue cooking over the boiling water until a candy thermometer registers 260°. Immediately add the nuts, citron, and orange rind.

Pour the mixture into the lined loaf pans about ½-inch deep, or deep enough to slightly cover the hazelnuts. Cover the top with the Ostia and cool for 45 minutes.

Cut into 1- to 2-inch squares to serve.

PANETTONE

1 ENVELOPE ACTIVE
DRY YEAST
5 CUPS SIFTED CAKE
FLOUR
1½ CUPS WARM
WATER
¾ CUP MELTED
UNSALTED
BUTTER
6 LARGE EGG YOLKS
2 WHOLE LARGE
EGGS
1 CUP SUGAR
½ CUP YELLOW
RAISINS
½ CUP FINELY
CHOPPED CANDIED
CITRON
1 TABLESPOON
UNSALTED
BUTTER

SERVES 12

Dissolve the yeast in 2 tablespoons of warm water and let it stand for 15 minutes.

Work ½ cup of the sifted cake flour into the yeast. Form the mixture into a ball and place it in a buttered bowl. Cover and let it rise for 2 hours, or until the dough has doubled in volume.

Place 2 cups of the sifted cake flour on a pastry board and make a mound with a well in the center. Place the dough ball in the well and slowly add about ⅔ cup (or enough) water to knead the mixture into a large, soft ball. Return it to the buttered bowl. Cover and let it rise for 2 hours, or until it doubles in volume.

Continue kneading, adding in the remaining flour and melted butter. Let it stand for 5 minutes.

Preheat the oven to 400°.

Beat together the egg yolks, whole eggs, sugar, and ½ cup water and knead this into the dough. When well combined, knead in the raisins and citron.

Place the dough in a greased and floured panettone pan and bake for 5 minutes. Remove it from the heat, cut a mark in the top of the loaf, and insert the 1 tablespoon of butter. Lower the oven to 375° and bake for 30 minutes more, or until golden. Cool on a wire rack and then remove the bread from the pan.

Panettone.

STIACCIATA

Generously butter four cookie sheets.

Dissolve the yeast in the warm water and let it stand for 5 minutes. Place the flour in a large bowl and slowly work the yeast mixture into it. Slowly add enough additional water to make a soft dough that does not stick to the sides of the bowl. When the dough is well kneaded, cover it with a dry cloth and let it stand for about 1 hour, or until doubled in volume.

Deflate the dough and knead in the eggs, salt, and 1 cup of the confectioners' sugar. When well combined, begin kneading in the butter until it is all absorbed.

Form the dough into 2-inch balls and place them on the prepared cookie sheets. Cover with a dry cloth and let them rise for 2 hours.

Preheat the oven to 400° and bake the risen dough for 30 minutes, or until golden. Remove the stiacciata from the heat and cool them on wire racks. Generously dust them with the remaining confectioners' sugar.

2 PACKETS ACTIVE DRY YEAST
½ CUP WARM WATER
5 CUPS SIFTED ALL-PURPOSE FLOUR
2 LARGE EGGS
¼ TEASPOON SALT
1½ CUPS CONFECTIONERS' SUGAR
2 CUPS UNSALTED BUTTER, SOFTENED

SERVES 12

A Halloween Gathering

CREAM OF CHESTNUT SOUP

ROAST LOIN OF PORK STUFFED WITH APPLES
AND PRUNES

POTATOES WITH CHEDDAR AND HORSERADISH

BRUSSELS SPROUTS VINAIGRETTE

CELERY ROOT REMOULADE

SAGE BISCUITS

PUMPKIN MOUSSE IN JACK-O'-LITTLES

New Orleans has Mardi Gras, Rio de Janeiro has Carnevale, and New York City has the Greenwich Village Halloween Parade. The parade draws over 100,000 participants, each one in a costume more lavish and imaginative than the last.

The Halloween parade is followed by hundreds of costume parties where—behind the masks—age, personalities, and identities can be reshaped for an evening. Hosts strive to create an atmosphere in which their guests will feel free to release their inhibitions. Parties take on a harmony of their own, made out of the cacophony of ghosts, emperors, pixies, and fops.

A still life of Pumpkin Mousse in Jack-O'-Littles.

CREAM OF CHESTNUT SOUP

¼ CUP BUTTER

1 ½ CUPS CHOPPED ONION

2 POUNDS FRESH CHESTNUTS, SHELLED

2 CARROTS, CHOPPED

4 CUPS FRESH CHICKEN STOCK (SEE PAGE 37)

1 ½ CUPS LIGHT CREAM

½ CUP SHERRY

SALT AND PEPPER TO TASTE

¼ CUP CREME FRAICHE

SERVES 12

Heat the butter in a heavy saucepan over medium heat. Add the onion. Lower the heat and sauté for about 3 minutes, or until soft. Add the chestnuts, carrots, and Chicken Stock. Simmer, stirring occasionally, for 20 minutes, or until the chestnuts and carrots are soft. Remove from the heat.

Purée the chestnut mixture in a blender or food processor. Strain it into a clean saucepan. Add the light cream, sherry, and salt and pepper to taste and bring to a simmer, stirring constantly. Remove the soup from the heat and pour it into the serving bowls. Garnish with a dollop of crème fraîche, if desired.

ROAST LOIN OF PORK STUFFED WITH APPLES AND PRUNES

1 7-POUND WELL-TRIMMED PORK LOIN

2 RED DELICIOUS APPLES

1 POUND PITTED PRUNES

1 ¼ CUPS CALVADOS

¼ CUP UNSALTED BUTTER

2 CUPS CHOPPED ONION

SALT AND PEPPER TO TASTE

SERVES 12

Using a knife or reaming device, make a 1-inch diameter hole down the center of the loin. Set it aside.

Peel, core, and dice the apples. Cut the prunes in half. Place the diced apples, prunes, and Calvados in a bowl. Set them aside to marinate for at least 30 minutes.

Preheat the oven to 375°.

Melt the butter in a heavy saucepan over medium heat. Add the onion and cook, stirring frequently, for about 15 minutes, or until the onion begins to caramelize. Add a bit of Calvados from the marinade to deglaze the pan. Add the caramelized onion and any pan juices to the apples and prunes and mix to combine.

Drain the mixture (reserving the marinade) and stuff it into the loin. Use the reserved marinade to coat the loin. Sprinkle it with salt and pepper to taste. Place the loin on a rack in a roasting pan and roast for 1 hour and 15 minutes, or until a meat thermometer registers 180°.

Slice the loin and serve it with any pan juices.

Guests bring the color to every costume event.

86

Roast Loin of Pork Stuffed with Apples and Prunes.

POTATOES WITH CHEDDAR AND HORSERADISH

12 LARGE POTATOES
½ CUP MILK
½ CUP UNSALTED BUTTER
SALT AND PEPPER TO TASTE
1½ TABLESPOONS PREPARED HORSERADISH

1 CUP WHIPPED CREAM
½ CUP GRATED CHEDDAR
HUNGARIAN PAPRIKA

SERVES 12

Preheat the oven to 350°.

Peel and cube the potatoes. Cook them in lightly salted water over medium high heat for about 15 minutes, or until tender. Drain.

Whip the potatoes in an electric mixer with the milk and butter until fluffy. Season them with salt and pepper and fold in the horseradish.

Pour the mixture into a lightly buttered 8-inch-square baking dish. Cover it with the whipped cream and sprinkle with cheese. Sprinkle the top with paprika.

Bake for 20 minutes, or until the top is lightly browned.

BRUSSELS SPROUTS VINAIGRETTE

3 PINTS BRUSSELS SPROUTS
¼ CUP SALTED BUTTER
1½ CUPS DRY WHITE WINE
SALT AND PEPPER TO TASTE
DIJON VINAIGRETTE

SERVES 12

Peel any damaged leaves from the Brussels sprouts. Trim the ends and cut a cross into the clean end. Place them in water to cover and bring to a boil over medium heat. Lower the heat and simmer for 10 minutes, or until the Brussels sprouts are cooked but still firm and bright green. Immediately place them in cold water. When they are cool, drain and pat them dry.

Melt the butter in a heavy sauté pan over medium heat. Add the Brussels sprouts and wine and salt and pepper to taste. Lower the heat and sauté for about 4 minutes, or until the Brussels sprouts are nicely glazed.

Remove the mixture from the heat and toss in the Dijon Vinaigrette. Serve at room temperature.

An easy and appetizing vegetable vinaigrette for fall.

DIJON VINAIGRETTE

1 TABLESPOON UNSALTED BUTTER
1 TABLESPOON MINCED SHALLOTS
½ CUP DRY WHITE WINE

1 CUP MAYONNAISE
⅓ CUP DIJON MUSTARD
SALT AND PEPPER TO TASTE

Melt the butter in a small sauté pan over medium heat. Add the shallots and cook, stirring frequently, for about 3 minutes, or until the shallots are soft. Add the wine and cook until it is reduced by two-thirds. Remove from the heat and allow to cool.

Whisk the shallot mixture into the mayonnaise. Add the mustard and salt and pepper, and whisk to combine.

CELERY ROOT REMOULADE

3 POUNDS CELERY ROOT

½ LEMON

3 CUPS FRESH CHICKEN STOCK (SEE PAGE 37)

3 TABLESPOONS CORN OIL

1 ½ TEASPOONS WHITE WINE VINEGAR

SALT AND PEPPER TO TASTE

¼ CUP FRESH TARRAGON LEAVES

½ CUP WATERCRESS LEAVES

10 FRESH CHIVES

1 TABLESPOON CHOPPED FRESH PARSLEY

1 TABLESPOON MINCED FRESH GARLIC

1 TEASPOON DIJON MUSTARD

1 ½ CUPS MAYONNAISE

SERVES 12

Peel and julienne the celery root. Place the lemon in a bowl of cold water and add the julienned celery root to keep it from turning brown.

Place the Chicken Stock in a heavy saucepan over medium heat. Drain the celery root and add it. Lower the heat and cook for about 4 minutes, or until the celery root is slightly cooked but still crisp. Drain.

Whisk together the corn oil, vinegar, and salt and pepper to taste. Stir this into the celery root. Cover and refrigerate for at least 4 hours.

In a food processor, using the metal blade, purée the tarragon, watercress, chives, parsley, and garlic. Stir in the mustard and mayonnaise.

Blend the celery root and mayonnaise mixtures and serve immediately.

Celery Root Remoulade with Sage Biscuits.

Pumpkin Mousse in Jack-O'-Littles.

SAGE BISCUITS

Preheat the oven to 450°.

Sift together the flour, salt, baking powder, and sugar.

In a food processor, using the metal blade, combine all the ingredients until the dough pulls away from the side of the bowl. (You may need up to ¼ cup more flour.)

Roll the dough out on a lightly floured board to ½-inch thick. Cut it with a floured 2-inch biscuit cutter.

Place the biscuits on an ungreased baking sheet, allowing the biscuits to touch. Bake them for 12 to 15 minutes, or until just golden.

2 CUPS ALL-PURPOSE FLOUR
½ TEASPOON SALT
4 TEASPOONS BAKING POWDER
¼ CUP SUGAR
⅔ CUP MILK
½ CUP VEGETABLE SHORTENING
8 LEAVES OF FRESH SAGE, CHOPPED

SERVES 12

PUMPKIN MOUSSE IN JACK-O'-LITTLES

1½ CUPS HEAVY CREAM
5 TABLESPOONS SOUR CREAM
7 LARGE EGG YOLKS
1 TEASPOON GROUND DRIED GINGER
¼ TEASPOON GROUND CLOVES
½ TEASPOON GROUND CINNAMON
½ CUP SUGAR
2½ TABLESPOONS LIGHT RUM
½ TEASPOON VANILLA EXTRACT

Blend the heavy cream and the sour cream. Cover and refrigerate for at least 1 hour.

Using an electric mixer, whip together the yolks, spices, sugar, rum, and vanilla until thick and pale yellow. Stir in the well-drained pumpkin purée and the lemon rind until well blended. Cover and refrigerate for at least 30 minutes.

Using an electric mixer, beat the chilled heavy cream mixture. When it is stiff, fold in the dissolved gelatin. Fold the cream into the chilled pumpkin mixture. Cover and refrigerate for at least 1 hour.

Cut the tops off of each miniature pumpkin to make a neat lid. Carve out the insides and discard. Wash and drain the shells well. Pat the insides dry.

When the pumpkin shells are dry, fill them with the chilled pumpkin mousse. Sprinkle the tops with the chopped crystallized ginger and garnish them with orange zests. Serve each jack-o'-little on a small dessert plate, with the top balanced at the side.

2½ CUPS CANNED PUMPKIN PUREE, WELL DRAINED
½ TEASPOON GRATED FRESH LEMON RIND
2 TEASPOONS UNFLAVORED GELATIN DISSOLVED IN 1 TABLESPOON COLD WATER
12 MINIATURE PUMPKINS
2 TABLESPOONS CHOPPED CRYSTALLIZED GINGER
12 ORANGE ZESTS

SERVES 12

A Corporate Sponsorship

DEVILED CRAB WITH SPICY MADELEINES

LAMB MERLOT

BROCCOLI WITH STAR FRUIT

RED AND WHITE SPAETZLE

CLASSIC SHORTBREAD

CHOCOLATE CONES WITH BERRIES AND
TROPICAL FRUIT SAUCE

When the exhibition of the works of Frederic Remington opened at The Metropolitan Museum of Art, the corporation sponsoring the show's national tour wanted to celebrate. They aptly choose The American Wing at the Met to stage a lavish dinner. The spirit of the burgeoning West as depicted by Remington seemed to perfectly reflect the host's leadership and pioneering commitment to art.

For the evening, we transformed the central courtyard into a dining room from the Golden Age. Biographical material describing Remington's zest for dining inspired the decor and the menu. Servers wore costumes of the period, while the velvet-covered chairs, cascading grapes, and soft candlelight added to the lushness of the evening.

This celebration truly bespoke of the corporation's commitment to public service, its adventurous spirit, and its appreciation of art.

The splendor of style.

Golden and bubbling Deviled Crab with Spicy Madeleines.

DEVILED CRAB
WITH SPICY MADELEINES

1 ½ TABLESPOONS
   SALTED BUTTER
⅓ CUP MINCED
   FRESH CELERY
⅓ CUP MINCED
   FRESH GREEN
   PEPPERS
⅓ CUP MINCED ONION
⅓ CUP MINCED
   SCALLIONS
½ TEASPOON MINCED
   FRESH GARLIC
1 TABLESPOON
   CREOLE MUSTARD
1 ½ TEASPOONS
   WORCESTERSHIRE
   SAUCE

Preheat oven to 375°.

Melt the butter in a sauté pan over medium heat. Add the celery, green peppers, onion, scallions, and garlic, and cook for 1 minute or just until the vegetables sweat. Cool and mix with the mustard, Worcestershire sauce, Tabasco, peppers, and egg. Fold into the crab meat.

Fill 1½ x 3-inch ramekins. Top with a spoonful of heavy cream and cover the top evenly with mayonnaise. Sprinkle with the paprika. Place ramekins on a baking sheet and bake for about 5 minutes or until golden and bubbling.

Serve hot, with Spicy Madeleines.

½ TEASPOON
   TABASCO SAUCE
BLACK AND WHITE
   PEPPER TO TASTE
CAYENNE PEPPER TO
   TASTE
1 LARGE EGG
¾ POUND LUMP CRAB
   MEAT, CLEANED
⅓ CUP HEAVY CREAM
⅓ CUP MAYONNAISE
1 TEASPOON
   HUNGARIAN
   PAPRIKA

SERVES 12

SPICY MADELEINES

¼ CUP SALTED
   BUTTER,
   SOFTENED
⅓ CUP MILK
1 LARGE EGG
¼ CUP YELLOW
   CORNMEAL
½ CUP ALL-PURPOSE
   FLOUR

Preheat oven to 425°.

Melt the butter and use 2 tablespoons to brush the madeleine pans. Whisk together the milk and remaining butter and egg. Stir the remaining ingredients into the milk mixture. Blend well.

Spoon into the prepared pans and bake for 12 minutes, or until the edges begin to pull away from the pans and the madeleines are golden. Serve warm.

½ TEASPOON BAKING
   POWDER
¼ TEASPOON DRIED
   BASIL
⅛ TEASPOON PEPPER
⅓ CUP GRATED
   FONTINA CHEESE

Lamb Merlot, Broccoli with Starfruit, and Red and White Spaetzle.

LAMB MERLOT

¾ CUP LIGHT SOY
   SAUCE
¾ CUP SESAME OIL
¾ CUP OLIVE OIL
4 STALKS CELERY,
   CHOPPED
2 TABLESPOONS
   FRESH MINCED
   GARLIC
1 TABLESPOON
   FRESH MINCED
   ROSEMARY

¾ TEASPOON FRESH
   MINCED OREGANO
1 ½ TEASPOONS DRY
   MUSTARD
3 RACKS OF LAMB
1 ½ CUP RED TABLE
   WINE

SERVES 12

Combine the soy sauce, sesame oil, olive oil, celery, garlic, herbs, and mustard. Stir to blend.

Place the racks of lamb in a non-reactive pan and pour the soy marinade on top. Cover and refrigerate for at least 8 hours, turning frequently.

Preheat oven to 450°.

Drain the lamb, saving the marinade. Place the lamb on wire racks in a roasting pan. Roast for 20 minutes, basting frequently, or until the lamb tests medium rare on a meat thermometer. Remove from the heat.

While the lamb is roasting, strain the marinade into a saucepan and cook over medium high heat. Add the wine and let it boil for 15 minutes or until the liquid reduces to one-third. When the lamb is done, slice it into serving portions and drizzle the warm marinade over the top.

BROCCOLI WITH STARFRUIT

3 LARGE HEADS OF
   BROCCOLI
4 STARFRUIT
½ CUP SALTED
   BUTTER
SALT AND PEPPER
   TO TASTE

SERVES 12

Cut the broccoli into small florets. Set aside the stems for another use. Place the florets in rapidly boiling salted water for 3 minutes or until they are bright green but still crisp. Immediately place them in ice water. When cool, drain them and pat dry.

Cut the starfruit crosswise into 36 slices, retaining the star shape.

Heat the butter in a heavy sauté pan over medium heat. Add the broccoli and salt and pepper and sauté for 1 minute. Place starfruit on top and cook for 1 more minute. Serve immediately.

RED AND WHITE SPAETZLE

5½ CUPS
ALL-PURPOSE
FLOUR
1 TEASPOON SALT
¼ TEASPOON PEPPER
¼ TEASPOON
GROUND NUTMEG
9 LARGE EGGS
1½ CUPS MILK
1½ CUPS HEAVY
CREAM
1½ TABLESPOONS
TOMATO PASTE
½ CUP UNSALTED
BUTTER
SALT AND PEPPER
TO TASTE

SERVES 12

In a large bowl, combine the flour, salt, pepper, and nutmeg. Form a well in the flour and add the eggs and ¾ cup of milk. Beat the eggs with a fork to blend with the milk. Then stir in the flour, pulling it into the center from the sides of the well. Whisk until smooth. Gradually whisk in the remaining milk and the cream.

Divide the dough into two bowls, adding the tomato paste to one. Cover with a dry towel and let it stand at room temperature for 30 minutes.

Bring a large pot of salted water to a boil. Place a bowl of cold water next to the boiling water. Hold a colander over the boiling water and pour in about 1 cup of the spaetzle batter. Use a rubber spatula to force the batter through the holes. When the spaetzle float to the top of the water, scoop them out with a slotted spoon or skimmer. Immediately transfer them to the cold water. Repeat with the remaining batter. When all the spaetzle are cooked, drain very well.

Melt the butter over high heat in a large sauté pan. When the butter separates, add the spaetzle and sauté over medium heat for about 10 minutes, tossing frequently, until heated through and golden. Season with salt and pepper and serve immediately.

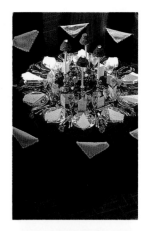

Costumed servers lend an air of authenticity to a historic theme.

CLASSIC SHORTBREAD

1 CUP UNSALTED
BUTTER
½ CUP SUPER-FINE
SUGAR
1 TEASPOON
VANILLA EXTRACT
2 CUPS ALL-
PURPOSE FLOUR
¼ CUP CORNSTARCH

SERVES 12

Preheat oven to 300°.

Cream together the butter and sugar until light and fluffy. Stir in the vanilla.

Sift together the flour and cornstarch, and gradually blend with the creamed mixture until combined.

Divide the dough in half and pat each portion into a 9-inch pie tin, carefully smoothing the edges and top. Crimp edges with your fingers as for a pie. Using the tines of a fork, section the shortbread into 8 equal wedges.

Place in oven and bake for 30 minutes or until the center is firm and the top is just golden.

Remove from the oven and cool on a wire rack for 10 minutes. Cut through the sections with a sharp knife and finish cooling.

Berries and Tropical Fruit Sauce embellish luxurious Chocolate Cones.

CHOCOLATE CONES WITH BERRIES AND TROPICAL FRUIT SAUCE

Cut 12 pieces of waxed paper to fit the inside of 12 2-inch diameter metal pastry cones.

Using a pastry brush, generously coat the inside of the metal pastry cones with vegetable oil. Fit the waxed paper cones into the oiled inside of each pastry cone.

Melt the chocolate in the top half of a double boiler over boiling water. When melted, remove the pan from the heat, keeping the chocolate warm while working with it.

Using a clean pastry brush, generously coat the inside of each prepared cone with the warm chocolate, making certain that the pointed end is well coated.

When each cone has been coated, refrigerate the cones for 2 hours. Then brush the insides again with the warm chocolate. Let the cones set for 1 hour or until the chocolate is quite hard. Remove each chocolate cone from its metal cone and carefully peel off the waxed paper. Set aside.

Gently toss together all of the clean berries.

Coat the bottom of each dessert plate with Tropical Fruit Sauce. Fill each cone with the mixed berries and lay it in the center of each plate, allowing the berries to spill out. If necessary, add additional berries to make an attractive arrangement. Garnish with a sprig of mint and serve immediately.

¼ CUP VEGETABLE OIL

2½ POUNDS GLAZING CHOCOLATE

2 CUPS WASHED, DRIED AND HULLED RASPBERRIES

2 CUPS VERY SMALL, WASHED, DRIED AND HULLED STRAWBERRIES (IF POSSIBLE, USE *FRAIS DE BOIS*)

2 CUPS BLUEBERRIES, WASHED AND DRIED

2 CUPS WASHED, DRIED AND HULLED BLACKBERRIES

TROPICAL FRUIT SAUCE

SERVES 12

A concept should be carried out down to the smallest detail.

TROPICAL FRUIT SAUCE

Peel the papaya, mango, kiwi, banana, and passion fruit. Purée together in a food processor using the metal blade. Press through a fine sieve to remove any fibers. Add the lemon juice and set aside.

Bring the sugar and water to a boil in a small saucepan over high heat. Add the liqueur and boil for 2 minutes. Remove from the heat and cool.

Combine the fruit purée and sugar syrup in a food processor using the metal blade. Cover and refrigerate until ready to use.

2 PAPAYA

2 MANGO

1 KIWI

1 BANANA

1 PASSION FRUIT

2 TABLESPOONS FRESH LEMON JUICE

½ CUP SUGAR

½ CUP WATER

3 TABLESPOONS PASSION FRUIT LIQUEUR

WHEN *and* WHERE

DECIDING ON THE RIGHT TIME TO GIVE A PARTY IS NOT AS SIMPLE AS IT MAY APPEAR AT FIRST. The "when" of a celebration refers both to its scheduled time of day and also to the time of year. But you should also consider the time it will require from you. Timing is often determined by the purpose of the event yet just as often the chosen time dictates the type of party.

If you entertain frequently, it is wise to sketch out a calendar of events at the beginning of the year. Take careful stock of your time and abilities, choosing to entertain only as frequently as your financial and emotional reserves will allow. There is nothing more uninviting than an overextended host. Remember that the busiest time on the social calendar occurs between September and June. And if you are planning an event during the particularly social season from Thanksgiving through New Year's, be certain to give your guests at least six weeks' notice.

In choosing the time of day for your party, the following generally accepted rules of entertaining etiquette may be helpful:

Timing and place must be harmoniously coordinated.

Time	Type of Party	Dress
7 to 10 A.M.	Breakfast	Semiformal to casual
10 to 11 A.M.	Coffee	Semiformal
10 A.M. to 5 P.M.	Brunch	Casual
12 to 3 P.M.	Luncheon	Semiformal to casual
4 to 6 P.M.	Tea	Semiformal
3 to 7 P.M.	Tea dance	Semiformal to black tie
5 to 9 P.M.	Cocktails	Semiformal to casual
6 to 10 P.M.	Extended cocktails or evening brunch	Semiformal
7 P.M. on	Dinner or dinner dance	White or black tie to semiformal
10 P.M. on	Supper or supper dance	White or black tie to semiformal

If an event demands a particular attire, be sure to note this on the invitation.

Breakfast: Almost exclusively in the domain of corporate entertaining, breakfasts allow the host to take advantage of the fact that the demands of the day have not yet begun. Important deals are often established over intimate, early morning breakfasts, and productive staff meetings can take place over a morning meal.

In your home, breakfasts for weekend guests can be much more casual. Set the meal up buffet style so that your guests can be on a flexible schedule. A typical menu would include two courses, coffee or tea, and often an eye-opener, such as a Bloody Mary, screwdriver, or mimosa.

Coffee: For informal, private get-togethers or for volunteer meetings, coffee is an excellent way to unite a group that is not on a 9–to–5 schedule. No alcohol is offered, and either sweets or a light snack are served. Two hours is the optimum time that should be allowed for such a get-together.

Brunch: This pleasant, casual affair is usually reserved for weekends or holidays, when people want to begin their day in a relaxed fashion. State the beginning and ending times clearly, since a brunch can easily extend through the day. Offer a selection of foods and drink appropriate for both breakfast and lunch, and serve alcohol if you choose.

Luncheon: Less formal than dinners, luncheons are adaptable to many situations—from business to pleasure. Lunch may consist of two or three courses, with one wine, if desired. At a small luncheon, the host can serve, but if there are more than twenty people, you should hire service personnel. Unless accompanied by a show or extended presentation, luncheons shouldn't last more than an hour and a half. This midday break is just that—a break in the day's activities, not a disruption in the guests' normal schedule.

Tea: A tea is the perfect party to entertain a broad age group, when liquor-only would not be appropriate. Or a tea may be given for just one guest, with great style and comfort. Serve an array of light food. The event should last about two hours.

Tea Dance: The goal of a late afternoon tea dance is usually to transport guests at a private celebration to a time gone by. A light buffet and alcohol can be served in place of tea and coffee. The party should last no more than three hours.

Cocktails: As corporate entertainment, cocktail parties are perfect for dealing with large groups when intimate host-guest contact is not expected but business is still important. For entertaining friends, cocktails encourage a relaxed interaction without the demands of a full, formal meal. Cocktail parties may be the at-home prelude to a more formal event in another location or to an evening on the town. They are frequently used in fund-raising or as a way for volunteers to meet their corporate sponsors.

Plan to serve cocktails for no more than three hours, encouraging guests to feel free to come and go at their leisure. Offer hors d'oeuvres ranging from light finger foods to elegantly prepared delicacies; they should always be easy to eat in two

TOP *A spring wedding luncheon, naturally, outdoors.*
ABOVE *A corporate cocktail bash in a disco.*

bites at the most and slightly salty or spiced to tease the palate. If you hire a butler, have him serve hors d'oeuvres on beautifully garnished trays, with cocktail napkins as "plates." For a cocktail buffet, display foods on a platter or in chafing dishes for self-service or service by waiters. Offer small plates and cocktail forks if the food is substantial. Dispense drinks from a bar or serve them on trays.

Extended Cocktails or Evening Brunch: These parties are variations on the standard cocktail party, except that more substantial foods are served.

Dinner or Dinner Dance: Begin a dinner or dinner dance with cocktail service if you wish, but for no more than forty-five minutes. If the dinner is purely social, allow time to linger over each course, with relaxing periods in between. Ensure a pleasant flow to the evening by serving coffee away from the dining table.

When serving dinner at a corporate or public function, move things along rapidly: The entire event should run no more than three hours. If a presentation is being made or an honor given, this should occur after dessert is served. If dancing is scheduled, start it when people enter the dining-room, continuing between courses and at the end of the meal.

Serve a dinner of at least three courses, with the appropriate wines. A formal, seated dinner calls for five courses, with changes in wines for each course, and the use of service personnel. A buffet can be either self-served or served by waiters. Plan a broad choice of foods, with desserts at a separate table or served by waiters to the guests' tables. At large dinners, you may continue to dispense drinks from a bar, but serve wines at the individual tables.

Supper or Supper Dance: Similar to but less formal than a dinner or dinner dance, suppers call for lighter menus and a more relaxed atmosphere. Late suppers are often held after an evening at the theater or an art opening.

Frequently, you entertain in order to celebrate a specific event—a wedding, a corporate merger, a first major benefit. Try to use your imagination in defining the party as well as in designing it so the event involves all those who may be touched by the occasion. At the birth of a baby, for example, organize a party for the new

Even in winter, your home can be extended with the use of a tent.

mother, pampering her with personal gifts such as pretty clothing, perfume, and lacy lingerie. Or, you could host a congratulatory dinner for the proud grandparents. Think about the many possible ways to celebrate an occasion and you'll come up with some unique ideas.

Weddings will be perhaps the most lavish entertainment you have to plan, and the most anxiety-producing. To allow yourself to actually enjoy the event, begin planning at least six months in advance. Weddings usually mean a whole season of milestones: engagement parties, bridal showers, bachelor parties, rehearsal dinners, and, finally, the wedding itself—with its ensuing reception. All of this is to be accomplished with the cooperation and understanding of two individuals, two different families, and sometimes even two different cultures.

Traditionally, the major expense of a wedding falls on the family of the bride. But times, relationships, and economics nowadays permit as many alternatives as you can imagine. The bride and groom always have their own vision of this special day, and whoever serves as host must demonstrate great diplomacy to integrate their expectations with the divergent interests of the families and friends.

In scheduling a wedding, take into account the comfort of the invited guests. Consider how far they will be traveling, whether they'll be staying overnight, and where, and how many cars may be needed. Whatever events you plan, space them so that the prenuptial festivities don't overtax the participants or outshine the wedding itself.

Holidays are perfect occasions to share with friends and acquaintances you'd like to know better. They are a time to celebrate with people of all ages—children on school breaks, friends home to visit family, and business associates with whom you want to establish a closer relationship. These occasions become the threads of our lives; they are markers in our memory and become the framework for who we are.

For corporate functions, bear in mind that these business parties are statistically best attended when held Monday through Thursday. Keep the number of speakers to a minimum and the speeches to the

Locating the proper space to accomodate large numbers of guests is a challenge that always spurs creative solutions.

point. Arrange for dinners held during the work week to end no later than 11 P.M., to allow the guests travel time as well as a decent night's sleep. If you are hosting a cocktail party, remember that most business people have to drive to and from the workplace. Offer enough cocktail fare so that if a guest has to forego dinner, he can do so comfortably. Avoid planning business receptions on or around major holidays, when many of your corporate guests may want to use the free time to extend vacations. Outside of the Christmas and Chanukkah season, avoid associating corporate events with religious holidays. (One exception to this rule is when a product is inherently associated with a particular holiday.) National holidays, however, provide a good reason to celebrate corporate and national pride.

If you are planning a benefit or other fund-raising event, timing is crucial. Many charitable institutions have on-staff fund-raising personnel with years of experience, who can assist you in planning a public event. When deciding on a time, first find out what other organizations in town have scheduled the evening you prefer. Avoiding conflicts for your targeted guests is very important. Because volunteers' schedules can be so erratic, begin work for any major event one year in advance. Consider certain holidays as inspiration for a charitable event: a Valentine's Day dinner dance for the Heart Fund, a small reception around Thanksgiving to show appreciation to volunteers and benefactors.

All parties—private, corporate, or public—must have a defined beginning, middle, and end. Although you should always be open to spontaneity, a schedule worked out well in advance will help keep the party in motion. Decide what will be the highlight of the evening and when it should be reached as well as how soon after the highlight you'd like your guests to leave. Pace a dinner so that guests don't stay more than an hour after dessert—except for family or dear friends with whom you want to chat. The two most acceptable and effective ways to suggest a party's conclusion are to close the bar and to change the level of lighting.

Choosing the best place to give a party can be as challenging as deciding on the proper time for the event. Every location will lend its own spirit to a party. Whether it's a private home or a huge hall will influence your thoughts and help you decide on a final plan. Choose the location according to the type of event you wish to host. Consider size, physical surroundings, availability of service areas, ventilation, and parking. The cardinal rule is to be certain the location is compatible with your ideas about entertaining.

Accessibility is a must in choosing any place. If the location is more than five miles away from the guests, include travel instructions within the invitation. Make sure that parking and public or hired transportation are available, and let guests know of accessibility to the handicapped, if appropriate.

No matter what the purpose of the event, any space you choose must have two separate areas: one for greeting guests, and another for partying. The first can be as small as an entrance foyer, but it must allow guests a minute to be greeted warmly, remove their outerwear, dispense gifts, and embrace the spirit of the occasion. The space must hold your guests comfortably. Never overcrowd.

At very large receptions, it is important to mark the center of the activity. Use an existing architectural feature, such as a fountain or atrium, or create a centerpiece with an eye-catching floral or food arrangement.

Rented space need not be the most expensive item on your list. There are many halls for public rental, some belonging to schools or churches, others to private clubs or historic sites, often available at a reasonable fee on days or evenings when they are normally closed. If you want to provide your own food and service, be sure that the rental space does not insist on your using its kitchen or hiring

A quiet interior loggia lends its own spirit for cocktails.

its staff. On the other hand, you may welcome a location that will provide a caterer for you.

Outdoor spaces can offer lots of room at little or no cost. If you have a yard or a shared recreational area, partying outdoors will be a snap. But public spots also offer an almost limitless range of entertainment areas. However, the major drawback to outdoor entertaining is the unpredictability of the weather. When nature interferes the backup of a rented tent can save an outdoor event.

Children's parties cry for the freedom of the outdoors. A yard, complete with barbeque and pool, is perfect for a young people's party, but don't let not having the perfect set-up limit you. Skating rinks, zoos, museums, parks, playgrounds, bowling alleys, and sporting arenas, all offer pleasing party locations.

But children are not alone in enjoying the outdoors. Everyone can relish a barbeque held in a park pavilion or a tailgate picnic before or after a major sporting event.

Choose the space for a corporate party carefully. At a business function, guests do not want the same degree of physical intimacy as at private occasions. However, if the space is too large in relation to the number of guests, small impenetrable groups will form and networking will be impossible. Before making a choice, consider the architecture and interior design of the company's own headquarters. It presents an identity that you might want to maintain.

When selecting a space for a public occasion, make sure the location complements the charity, campaign, or institution. An unusual location can generate excitement, but it should never generate shock. A few public institutions are fortunate to be housed in magnificent buildings. If yours is, take advantage of the space. If not, search your community for appropriate public spaces.

One problem in using a dramatic space for a large public function is placing the guests so that they are impressed but not intimidated. Don't try to camouflage a large space; rather, focus attention down to the tabletops with lovely candles and flowers. The vastness will disappear in the guests' perception, but the mood of the space will persist.

Golden oldies are goodies.

Familiar landmarks make a memory-filled backdrop.

Whatever the space, plan the seating carefully. For eight to ten people, we prefer a 54- to 60-inch round table. Larger tables tend to destroy intimacy and isolate guests. Rectangular tables are less conducive to good conversation but can work if dinner partners are thoughtfully placed. If you are using buffet service, set the table apart from the area where guests will be seated for dining. If the buffet is self-service, place it in the center of the room, or anywhere that guests can walk around the table comfortably. This produces a natural flow and prevents lines.

If you are numbering tables for a dinner in a large space, put even numbers on one side of the room and odd on the other. Give the table farthest away from the entrance the lowest number and the table nearest, the highest. Place host and V.I.P. tables in the middle. These tactics simplify the seating of guests and create a less hierarchical organization of space.

Harmonious placement of guests for best social interaction is the mark of a great host. At an intimate gathering with one rectangular table, the host is usually seated at one end and the hostess at the other. The female guest of honor is to the right of the host; the male guest of honor to the right of the hostess. In Europe, to create a more intimate table, the host and hostess frequently sit opposite one another in the center of the rectangle. Either way, the dynamics of dining work best if no more than ten people are seated at a dining table.

If you are using round tables, put the host and hostess at separate tables. Also separate couples and old friends in order to stimulate conversation. At large parties or galas, place key personnel or celebrities at various tables throughout the room. Always use place cards to ensure the seating arrangement you prefer.

For buffets, make seating available for a large portion of the guests. It is sometimes practical to have formal seating, but it is just as acceptable to offer comfortable seating throughout your home or party space. Whatever you chose, be clear about

Buffet tables—whether served or self-served—should be easily accessible.

arrangements so that your guests are not left standing uncomfortably, balancing a plate and utensils.

When entertaining at home, use some ingenuity to offer table service in spaces not ordinarily used for dining. Card tables, collapsible and storable, covered with charming cloths are one way to expand dining areas. Clear the centers of rooms (you would be surprised how much can be hidden behind a shower curtain) and use every unmovable table or countertop to hold food, beverages, and flowers. Make a floor plan and stick to it.

The Chinese have a term, *feng shui*, which expresses the art of placement—harmonizing with your environment. As a host, if you master this art for yourself and your guests, memorable experiences will result.

A Greenhouse Dinner

LOBSTER SUPREME WITH WALNUT DRESSING

MEDALLIONS OF LAMB WITH BLACK BEAN
SAUCE

FIDDLEHEADS VINAIGRETTE

PINK BULGUR PILAF

DARK AND WHITE CHOCOLATE COEUR A LA
CREME WITH RASPBERRY SAUCE

Everyone always has a special place in their home where they feel most welcoming. Our hostess said she always gravitated to the greenhouse when giving guests a tour. Its placement on the grounds offered a splendid view of nature, and the changing light bathed the interior with warm tones as day moved into evening. It was a perfect location for the rehearsal luncheon and dinner for her son's wedding. Daylight brought a rainbow of hues, bouncing through the glass and onto the tabletops. When the guests returned for dinner, they found not only a change of fare, but the glorious colors of the sunset streaming into the area.

The greenhouse at twilight.

LOBSTER SUPREME
WITH WALNUT DRESSING

12 LOBSTER TAILS
⅔ CUP FRESH LEMON
    JUICE
1 CUP CORN OIL
½ CUP WALNUT OIL
1 TABLESPOON
    SUGAR
½ TEASPOON MINCED
    FRESH GARLIC

Place the lobster tails in rapidly boiling salted water. Cook them for 4 minutes, or until just done. Immediately plunge them into iced water to stop the cooking. Drain and cool them, then remove the tail meat in 1 piece.

Slice each tail into medallions, keeping the sections together in the tail's original form.

Whisk together the lemon juice, oils, sugar, garlic, and salt and pepper to taste and set aside.

Wash, drain, and dry the Mâche. Place equal portions on 12 salad plates. Fan out a lobster tail in the center of each plate. Drizzle it with the walnut dressing and sprinkle with chives.

SALT AND WHITE
    PEPPER TO TASTE
4 BUNCHES MACHE
    LETTUCE
½ CUP CHOPPED
    FRESH CHIVES

SERVES 12

MEDALLIONS OF LAMB
WITH BLACK BEAN SAUCE

2 LAMB LOINS,
    BONED
SALT AND PEPPER
    TO TASTE
BLACK BEAN SAUCE

SERVES 12

Preheat the oven to 500°.

Place the loins on a roasting rack in a roasting pan. Sprinkle them with salt and pepper to taste and roast for 10 minutes. Turn and roast for an additional 5 minutes, or until a meat thermometer reads 120° (for rare). Let the lamb set for 5 minutes. Slice it into medallions and serve it capped with Black Bean Sauce.

NOTE: INGREDIENTS
MARKED WITH AN AS-
TERISK (*) CAN BE
FOUND IN THE ORIEN-
TAL SECTIONS OF SU-
PERMARKETS,
SPECIALTY STORES
AND ORIENTAL
MARKETS.

BLACK BEAN SAUCE

1 RED PEPPER
1 TABLESPOON
    CORN OIL
2 TABLESPOONS
    MINCED FRESH
    GARLIC
2 TABLESPOONS
    GRATED FRESH
    GINGER ROOT
¼ CUP FERMENTED
    BLACK BEANS*
1 TABLESPOON
    COGNAC

Seed and dice the red pepper.

Heat the corn oil in a medium sauté pan over high heat. Lower the heat and stir in the garlic, ginger root, and red pepper. Sauté for about 2 minutes, or until just soft.

Rinse the beans and add them to the pan. Sauté an additional 2 minutes.

Add the cognac and sherry and cook for 5 minutes, or until the mixture is reduced by one half.

Add the Beef Stock and simmer for 10 minutes.

Dissolve the cornstarch in the cold water. Whisk it into the sauce and cook until slightly thickened. Add salt and pepper to taste and serve warm.

2 TABLESPOONS
    SHERRY
3 CUPS BEEF STOCK
2 TABLESPOONS
    CORNSTARCH
2 TABLESPOONS
    COLD WATER
SALT AND PEPPER
    TO TASTE

Medallions of Lamb with Black Bean Sauce.

BEEF STOCK

5 POUNDS BEEF
   BONES
2 LARGE ONIONS,
   CHOPPED
4 CARROTS,
   CLEANED AND
   CHOPPED
4 CELERY STALKS,
   CLEANED AND
   CHOPPED
1 CUP RED WINE
   (OPTIONAL; IF NOT
   USED, ADD MORE
   WATER)
2½ QUARTS WATER
4 CLOVES GARLIC

Preheat oven to 500°.

Rub the beef bones with oil. Roast the bones, onion, carrot, celery, and tomato in the oven for 30 minutes.

Place the browned ingredients in a large stock pot. Deglaze the roasting pan with the red wine and 1 cup of the water. Add the liquid to the stock pot.

Add the remaining ingredients and bring to a boil. Reduce the heat and simmer for approximately 3 hours or until the liquid is reduced by half. Skim the surface for any foam or residue. Remove the bones and discard.

Strain the stock through a double layer of cheese cloth. Discard all of the remaining solid ingredients. Cool.

4 SPRIGS ITALIAN
   PARSLEY
4 SPRIGS FRESH
   THYME (2
   TABLESPOONS DRIED
   THYME)
2 BAY LEAVES
½ TEASPOON BLACK
   PEPPERCORNS
½ POUND PLUM
   TOMATOES
¼ CUP OLIVE OIL OR
   VEGETABLE OIL

MAKES 1 QUART

FIDDLEHEADS VINAIGRETTE

2 POUNDS
   FIDDLEHEAD
   FERNS (FROZEN OR
   FRESH IN SPRING)
¼ CUP UNSALTED
   BUTTER
1 TABLESPOON
   MINCED FRESH
   GARLIC

2 TABLESPOONS RED
   WINE
½ TEASPOON MINCED
   FRESH OREGANO
SALT AND PEPPER
   TO TASTE

SERVES 12

Soak the fiddleheads in hot water about 15 minutes, or until softened. Remove the hairs with a gentle brush or by hand. Pat the ferns dry.

Melt the butter in a sauté pan over medium heat. Add the garlic and the fiddleheads and sauté for 5 minutes, or until the fiddleheads are just cooked. Remove the fiddleheads from the pan and keep them warm. Pour the red wine into the pan and swirl to deglaze it. Immediately pour the pan juices over the fiddleheads and season with oregano and salt and pepper. Serve hot.

PINK BULGUR PILAF

½ CUP SALTED
   BUTTER
3 CUPS BULGAR
   (CRACKED WHEAT)
½ CUP FINELY
   CHOPPED ONION
3 CUPS TOMATO
   JUICE
SALT AND PEPPER
   TO TASTE

SERVES 12

Preheat the oven to 375°.

Melt the butter, less 1 tablespoon, in a heavy sauté pan. Add the bulgur and sauté for 5 minutes.

Heat the remaining tablespoon of butter in a small sauté pan over medium heat. Add the onion and sauté it for about 4 minutes, or until golden. Stir the onion into the bulgur and add the tomato juice and salt and pepper to taste.

Place the pilaf in a covered casserole and bake it for 30 minutes.

Uncover the casserole, stir well, and bake the pilaf for an additional 10 minutes. Serve hot.

DARK AND WHITE CHOCOLATE COEUR A LA CREME WITH RASPBERRY SAUCE

2 OUNCES
   SEMISWEET
   CHOCOLATE
¾ POUND CREAM
   CHEESE
2 CUPS HEAVY
   CREAM
¾ CUP
   CONFECTIONERS'
   SUGAR

1 TEASPOON
   VANILLA EXTRACT
2 OUNCES WHITE
   CHOCOLATE
RASPBERRY SAUCE

SERVES 12

Melt the semisweet chocolate in the top half of a double boiler over boiling water.

Beat half of the cream cheese until it is light and fluffy. Add ½ cup of the heavy cream and beat until smooth. Beat in half of the sugar and vanilla. When it is well blended, add the melted chocolate.

Whip another ½ cup of the heavy cream and fold it into the chocolate mixture. Set aside.

Repeat the above process using the white chocolate.

When the chocolates are ready, line 12 coeur à la crème (small heart-shaped) molds with dampened cheesecloth making the

Dark and White Chocolate Coeur à la Crème with Raspberry Sauce.

pieces large enough to both line the mold and cover it. Carefully pour in both mousses at the same time, with each filling half of the mold. Cover the molds with the cheesecloth and place them on a rack in a ridged pan to drain. Refrigerate for at least 8 hours.

When the molds are well set, unmold them and place them on a serving platter that has been coated with Raspberry Sauce.

RASPBERRY SAUCE

1 CUP FROZEN
  RASPBERRIES
1 ½ TABLESPOONS
  SUPERFINE SUGAR

Purée the raspberries and strain them through a fine sieve. Stir in the sugar and kirschwasser. Refrigerate the sauce until ready to serve.

½ TABLESPOON
  KIRSCHWASSER

A Broadway Opening

CHOUCROUTE

CHICKEN NORMANDY

POMMES SAVOYARDES

HARICOTS VERTS WITH ROASTED GARLIC

BRAISED FENNEL AND LEEKS

HUGUENOT TORTE

GRAND MARNIER FIGS AND TANGERINES

The success of *Les Misérables* in London guaranteed an enormous turnout for the New York opening. We wondered how many people would be in the mood to party after seeing a show in which the main set is a sewer, the hero dies, and half the characters are killed in an insurrection. But one thousand did.

The hosts of this historic Broadway opening chose a space that echoed the excitement of the show. Draped in a tent of lights, the Seventh Regiment Armory in Manhattan was transformed into a place of mystery and drama. The menu and table decor offered a hint of the French Revolution, making the guests feel that they were part of the show's adventure.

The huge space of an armory comes alive with the excitement of opening night—Les Misérables.

CHOUCROUTE

6 CUPS SAUERKRAUT

3 TABLESPOONS
  OLIVE OIL

1½ CUPS CHOPPED
  ONION

2 GRANNY SMITH
  APPLES (OR ANY
  GREEN APPLE)

½ TEASPOON
  JUNIPER BERRIES

½ TEASPOON BLACK
  PEPPERCORNS

1 CUP DRY WHITE
  WINE

1 CUP FRESH BEEF
  STOCK (SEE PAGE
  111)

1 POUND SLAB
  BACON, CUBED

1 POUND SMOKED
  HAM, CUBED

1 TEASPOON
  KIRSCHWASSER

1 POUND SAUCISSON
  A L'AIL (GARLIC
  SAUSAGE)

SERVES 12

Wash the sauerkraut and squeeze it dry. Set it aside.

Heat the oil in a heavy casserole over medium heat. Add the onions, lower the heat, and sauté them for 5 minutes, or until the onions are soft.

Peel, core, and chop the apples. Add the apples and sauerkraut to the casserole.

Tie the juniper berries and peppercorns in a cheesecloth bag and add them to the casserole.

Pour in the wine and Beef Stock and stir to blend. If the liquid does not cover the sauerkraut, add equal parts of the wine and stock until it does.

Lower the heat and cook for 2 hours.

Blanch the bacon in simmering water for 15 minutes. Drain it well. Add the bacon and ham to the sauerkraut and simmer it for an additional hour. Stir in the kirschwasser. Cover and simmer for 30 minutes more.

Meanwhile, slice the saucisson à l'ail into bite-size pieces and sauté them over low heat for about 15 minutes, or until cooked.

Place the sauerkraut in a serving bowl and garnish it with the saucisson.

CHICKEN NORMANDY

6 POUNDS
  BONELESS
  CHICKEN BREASTS

1¾ CUPS FRESH
  CHICKEN STOCK
  (SEE PAGE 37)

4 CUPS APPLE CIDER

3 GRANNY SMITH
  APPLES (OR ANY
  GREEN APPLE)

2 CUPS WATER

1 TEASPOON FRESH
  LEMON JUICE

2 CUPS HEAVY
  CREAM

2 TABLESPOONS
  CALVADOS

SALT AND PEPPER
  TO TASTE

2 TABLESPOONS
  MINCED FRESH
  ITALIAN PARSLEY

¼ CUP CHOPPED
  WALNUTS

SERVES 12

Clean the chicken breasts of fat and cartilage and cut them into quarters lengthwise.

Bring the Chicken Stock to a boil over medium heat. Add 1 cup of the cider and the chicken. Poach for 10 minutes, or until the chicken is just cooked. Drain.

Wash and core the apples and slice them into quarters. Set them aside in a bowl filled with 2 cups of water and 1 teaspoon of lemon juice.

Bring the remaining 3 cups of cider to a boil in a heavy saucepan over medium heat. Lower the heat and cook it for 15 minutes, or until reduced by half.

In another saucepan, cook the heavy cream over medium heat for 15 minutes, or until it is reduced by half.

Flame the alcohol off of the Calvados and set it aside.

Strain the reduced cider and cream together and whisk in the Calvados. Add salt and pepper to taste.

Add the cooked chicken and drained, uncooked apples to the sauce. Cook over low heat for about 5 minutes, or until the flavors blend and the apples are slightly cooked.

When you are ready to serve, garnish the chicken with the chopped parsley and walnuts.

Choucroute, Chicken Normandy, and Roasted Garlic.

Roasted Garlic—aromatic and delicious.

Pommes Savoyardes

Pommes Savoyardes laced with crisp leeks and celery.

Preheat the oven to 375°

Peel the potatoes and cut them in half. Slice each half diagonally into 4 slices, but keep the slices together.

Pour the Chicken Stock, clarified butter, and half of the cream into a 9 x 12-inch baking pan. Sprinkle the minced leeks and celery over all.

Lay the sliced potato halves in the pan and pour the remaining cream on top. Sprinkle with salt and pepper. Cover and bake for about 45 minutes, or until the potatoes are tender. Serve each person 1 potato half, with the slices slightly fanned.

6 LARGE IDAHO
POTATOES
¼ CUP FRESH
CHICKEN STOCK
(SEE PAGE 37)
½ CUP CLARIFIED
BUTTER, WARMED
1 CUP HEAVY CREAM
¾ CUP MINCED
LEEKS, WHITE
PART ONLY
¼ CUP MINCED
CELERY
SALT AND PEPPER
TO TASTE

SERVES 12

Haricots Verts
with Roasted Garlic

Preheat the oven to 325°.

Clean and trim the haricots verts. Place them in rapidly boiling salted water and cook for about 30 seconds, or until the beans are bright green and still crisp. Immediately plunge them into iced water. When they are chilled, drain and pat them dry. Set aside.

With a sharp knife, cut off the tops of the heads of garlic to expose the cloves. Leave the heads whole and place them in a small roasting pan. Toss them with 2 tablespoons of the olive oil and salt and pepper to taste. Put the pan, uncovered, in the oven and roast, stirring occasionally, for 25 minutes, or until the garlic is tender and golden brown.

Heat the remaining olive oil in the sauté pan over medium heat. Add the haricots verts and toss to heat them through. Add salt and pepper to taste.

Serve the beans garnished with roasted garlic.

2 POUNDS FRESH
HARICOTS VERTS
(TINY GREEN BEANS)
1 POUND GARLIC,
WHOLE
¼ CUP OLIVE OIL
SALT AND PEPPER
TO TASTE

SERVES 12

BRAISED FENNEL AND LEEKS

½ CUP UNSALTED BUTTER
1 TABLESPOON MINCED FRESH SAGE
1 TABLESPOON FRESH LEMON JUICE
2 POUNDS LEEKS, WHITE PART ONLY

Preheat the oven to 375°.

Cream the butter, sage, and lemon juice with an electric mixer. Set aside.

Wash the leeks well. Dry and cut them into strips. Place them in the bottom of a 2-quart baking dish.

Wash the fennel. Drain and trim it and cut it into 2 x 3-inch strips. Place the strips on top of the leeks in the baking dish.

Pour the stock, sherry, and oil over the fennel. Cover the dish and bake for 30 minutes. With a slotted spoon, remove the vegetables to a serving dish and dot them with the butter mixture.

3 POUNDS FRESH FENNEL
2 CUPS CHICKEN STOCK (SEE PAGE 37)
⅓ CUP SHERRY WINE
2½ TABLESPOONS OLIVE OIL

SERVES 12

Huguenot Torte with Grand Marnier Figs and Tangerines.

HUGUENOT TORTE

3 GRANNY SMITH
APPLES (OR ANY
GREEN APPLE)
2 TABLESPOONS
UNSALTED
BUTTER
3 TABLESPOONS
DARK BROWN
SUGAR
1½ TABLESPOONS
RUM
3 EXTRA-LARGE
EGGS
1 CUP ALL-PURPOSE
FLOUR

Preheat the oven to 325°.

Peel, core, and chop the apples.

Heat the butter in a medium sauté pan over low heat. Add the apples, brown sugar, and rum and sauté for 5 minutes. Remove the mixture from the heat and allow to cool.

Beat the eggs until frothy and lemon-colored. Add the flour, sugar, baking powder, vanilla, and salt. Beat until well combined.

Fold in the apple mixture and 1¼ cups of the chopped pecans. Pour the mixture into a buttered 3-quart casserole and bake for 45 minutes, until crusty and golden brown.

Serve the torte warm, garnished with the whipped cream or dusted with confectioners' sugar, and topped with the chopped pecans.

2¼ CUPS SUGAR
2¼ TEASPOONS
BAKING POWDER
1½ TEASPOON
VANILLA EXTRACT
PINCH SALT
1½ CUPS CHOPPED
PECANS
1½ CUPS HEAVY
CREAM, WHIPPED
¼ CUP
CONFECTIONERS'
SUGAR

SERVES 12

GRAND MARNIER FIGS
AND TANGERINES

Preheat the oven to 375°.

Place the walnut halves on a baking sheet and roast them for 5 minutes, or until lightly toasted. Remove them from the oven and set aside.

Peel, segment, and devein the tangerines. Quarter the figs. Combine the toasted nuts, tangerine segments, and figs. Add the Grand Marnier and vanilla and stir to blend.

Cover and refrigerate the mixture for 24 hours, stirring occasionally. Serve at room temperature.

1 CUP WALNUT
HALVES
6 TANGERINES
1 POUND DRIED FIGS
1½ CUPS GRAND
MARNIER
¼ TEASPOON
VANILLA EXTRACT

SERVES 12

A 50s Cocktail Buffet

SHRIMP COCKTAIL

OYSTER PO' BOYS

CRAYFISH ETOUFFEE WITH DIRTY RICE

TURKEY TAMALES WITH RED CHILI SAUCE

FIREHOUSE CHILI

JICAMA, PEAR, AND WATERCRESS SALAD

FUDGE PIE

A Wall Street exchange that sits on the cutting edge of financial America wanted to shake up its image. So we helped them find a spot where their guests could really shake, rattle, and roll.

The hottest disco in town was hired to give them a blast from the past. Buffets laden with familiar food from the 50s, a soda shop where guests could sip sodas with a sweetie, and a simulated drive-in complete with cars and carhops all conspired to take the dealers in futures back to their not-too-distant past.

A blast from the past can drown out the pressures of today.

SHRIMP COCKTAIL

1 CUP CATSUP

1 TEASPOON FRESH LEMON JUICE

1 TABLESPOON WORCESTER-SHIRE SAUCE

2 TABLESPOONS GRATED HORSERADISH

Whisk together the catsup, lemon juice, Worcestershire sauce, and horseradish. Place the sauce in a small serving bowl.

Arrange the shrimp on a serving platter with the bowl of sauce in the center. Garnish with Lemon Flowers.

2 POUNDS SHRIMP, COOKED, PEELED, AND DEVEINED

6 LEMON FLOWERS (SEE PAGE 23)

SERVES 12

OYSTER PO' BOYS

1 PINT SHUCKED OYSTERS

1 CUP YELLOW CORNMEAL

1 TEASPOON CAJUN MAGIC (OR OTHER PREPARED CAJUN SEASONING)

2 LARGE EGGS

3 TABLESPOONS MILK

1 ¼ CUPS UNFLAVORED BREAD CRUMBS

1 BAGUETTE

¼ CUP MELTED SALTED BUTTER

2 CUPS VEGETABLE OIL

TABASCO SAUCE TO TASTE

SERVES 12

Drain the oysters well, reserving the liquid for another use. Blend the cornmeal and Cajun Magic. Set aside.

Whisk the eggs and milk to blend.

Dip the oysters one at a time in the seasoned cornmeal, then in the egg, and finally in the bread crumbs. Let them set a few minutes.

Preheat the oven to 350°

Slice the baguette in half lengthwise, as if for a sandwich. Remove the soft center and brush the remaining shell with the melted butter. Wrap the shell in foil and bake it for 5 minutes, or until quite hot. Remove it from the foil and cut it into 1½-inch-thick sections.

Heat the oil in a deep fryer and fry the coated oysters, a few at a time for 2 minutes, or until golden. Drain them on paper towels.

Place 1 oyster inside each bread section. Sprinkle it with Tabasco sauce to taste and serve immediately.

CRAYFISH ETOUFFEE WITH DIRTY RICE

1 ½ TEASPOONS SALT

1 TEASPOON CAYENNE PEPPER

½ TEASPOON WHITE PEPPER

½ TEASPOON BLACK PEPPER

½ TEASPOON DRIED BASIL, GROUND

¼ TEASPOON DRIED THYME, GROUND

⅓ CUP CORN OIL

¼ CUP ALL-PURPOSE FLOUR

Combine the salt, peppers, basil, and thyme and set aside.

Heat the oil in a heavy sauté pan over medium heat for 4 minutes, or until smoking. Whisk in the flour gradually and cook, stirring constantly, for about 5 minutes, or until dark red-brown. (*Be careful not to scorch the roux.*) Remove the pan from the heat and immediately stir in the onion, celery, peppers, and 1 teaspoon of the seasoned salt. Continue stirring until cool.

Bring 2 cups of Fish Stock to a boil in a medium saucepan over high heat. Gradually whisk in the cooled vegetable roux. Cook, stirring constantly, for about 3 minutes, until thickened.

Melt the butter in a heavy sauté pan over low heat. Add the crayfish tails and scallions and sauté for 3 minutes. Scrape the mixture into the sauce and stir to blend. Add the remaining seasoned salt and cook over low heat until hot.

Serve immediately with Dirty Rice.

¼ CUP CHOPPED ONION

¼ CUP CHOPPED CELERY

½ CUP CHOPPED GREEN PEPPERS

2 CUPS FISH STOCK

½ CUP UNSALTED BUTTER

1 ½ POUNDS CRAYFISH TAILS, COOKED AND CLEANED

¾ CUP CHOPPED SCALLIONS

DIRTY RICE

SERVES 12

Oyster Po' Boys with martinis neat.

FISH STOCK

2 POUNDS WASHED FISH BONES AND HEADS WITH GILLS REMOVED

4 CUPS COLD WATER

1 CUP DRY WHITE WINE (IF NOT USED, ADD MORE WATER)

3 SPRIGS ITALIAN PARSLEY

2 SPRIGS FRESH CHERVIL (1 TEASPOON DRIED CHERVIL)

2 BAY LEAVES

2 SPRIGS FRESH THYME (1 TABLESPOON DRIED THYME)

Place all of the ingredients in a stock pot. Bring them to a boil, then reduce the heat to a simmer. Skim the surface of any foam or residue.

Cook the stock for approximately 30 minutes. Overcooking may produce bitterness.

Strain through a double layer of cheese cloth. Discard the solid ingredients. Cool.

½ TEASPOON BLACK PEPPERCORNS

1 CLOVE

2 SHALLOTS OR 1 SMALL YELLOW ONION, CHOPPED

1 LEEK, WHITE PART ONLY, WASHED AND CHOPPED

1 CARROT, PEELED AND CHOPPED

NOTE: LOBSTER, CRAB, OR SHRIMP SHELLS MAY BE ADDED FOR MORE FLAVOR.

MAKES 1 QUART

Shrimp with cocktail sauce—a standard.

DIRTY RICE

3 TEASPOONS CAYENNE PEPPER

2 TEASPOONS BLACK PEPPER

2 TEASPOONS HUNGARIAN PAPRIKA

1½ TEASPOONS DRY MUSTARD

1½ TEASPOONS GROUND CUMIN

½ TEASPOON DRIED THYME

½ TEASPOON OREGANO

3 TABLESPOONS CORN OIL

¾ POUND CHICKEN GIZZARDS

⅛ POUND GROUND PORK

Mix the cayenne and black peppers, paprika, mustard, cumin, thyme, and oregano and set aside. Finely chop the gizzards.

Heat the oil in a heavy sauté pan over medium heat. Stir in the chopped gizzards, ground pork, and bay leaves and sauté for 10 minutes, or until brown. Stir in the seasoning mix. Add the onion, celery, green pepper, and garlic. Stir, scraping the bottom of the pan to release the brown bits.

Add the butter and chopped chicken livers and cook for 8 minutes.

Pour in ½ cup of the stock and cook to release the brown bits from the bottom of the pan. Add the rice and stir to coat.

Pour in the remaining stock. Cover and cook for 15 minutes, or until the rice is just about cooked. Remove the pan from the heat, uncover it, and let it stand for 10 minutes, or until the rice is tender. Remove the bay leaves and serve immediately.

3 BAY LEAVES

½ CUP CHOPPED ONION

¼ CUP MINCED GREEN CELERY

¾ CUP CHOPPED GREEN PEPPER

3 TEASPOONS MINCED FRESH GARLIC

3 TABLESPOONS UNSALTED BUTTER

½ POUND CHICKEN LIVERS, CHOPPED

3 CUPS FRESH CHICKEN STOCK (SEE PAGE 37)

1¼ CUPS WHITE RICE

SERVES 12

TURKEY TAMALES
WITH RED CHILI SAUCE

1 POUND FRESH TURKEY MEAT, CUBED

1 SMALL ONION, PEELED AND QUARTERED

2 CLOVES GARLIC

SALT AND PEPPER TO TASTE

2 TEASPOONS VEGETABLE SHORTENING

2 TABLESPOONS CHOPPED FROZEN NEW MEXICO ROASTED RED CHILIES (HOT OR MILD)*

¼ TEASPOON GROUND DRIED OREGANO

¼ TEASPOON GROUND CUMIN

1 TABLESPOON BLACK RAISINS

2 TEASPOONS PIGNOLI NUTS

¼ POUND DRY CORN HUSKS*

1¼ CUP MASA HARINA (CORNMEAL FLOUR)*

1½ TEASPOON SALT

½ CUP LARD

RED CHILI SAUCE

SERVES 12

NOTE: INGREDIENTS MARKED WITH AN ASTERISK (*) CAN BE FOUND IN MEXICAN OR SPANISH GROCERIES.

Place the turkey, onion, garlic, and salt and pepper in enough cold water to cover in a saucepan. Bring to a boil over medium heat. Lower the heat and simmer for 20 minutes, or until the turkey is done. Strain the turkey, onion, and garlic from the broth, reserving ¾ cup of the broth.

In a food processor, using the metal blade, chop the turkey, onion, and garlic until finely ground.

Melt the vegetable shortening in a sauté pan over medium heat. Add the ground turkey mixture, red chilies, oregano, cumin, raisins, pignoli nuts, and salt to taste. Stir to blend and add enough of the broth to make a moist filling. Set aside.

Open and clean the corn husks. Soak them in warm water to cover for 30 minutes.

Place the masa harina and salt in the bowl of a food processor. Using the metal blade, incorporate the lard into the masa harina. Slowly add the turkey broth to make a dough that is thick but spreadable. (If you need additional liquid, use water.)

Cut the softened corn husks so that they are at least 4 inches wide and 7 inches long. Spread the masa harina dough over the husks, leaving ½ inch at each side and 1½ inches at each end. This should take about 2 tablespoons of dough for each.

Place 1 tablespoon of the turkey down the center of the dough. Fold the sides of the husk together and pinch the dough to seal. Fold in the bottom and the top to make a tightly sealed packet.

Place the finished tamales in a steamer over boiling water and steam them for 1 hour. Remove them from the steamer and carefully pull away the husks.

Serve warm, covered with Red Chili Sauce.

RED CHILI SAUCE

6 CUPS FROZEN NEW MEXICO ROASTED RED CHILIES*

1 LARGE TOMATO, PEELED AND SEEDED

3 CLOVES FRESH GARLIC

3 TEASPOONS GROUND DRIED OREGANO

1 TEASPOON GROUND CUMIN

4 CUPS COLD WATER

In a food processor, using the metal blade, purée the chilies, tomato, garlic, oregano, cumin, and 2 cups of the water.

Pour the mixture into a heavy saucepan. Add the remaining water and bring to a boil over high heat. Lower the heat and simmer for about 1 hour, or until reduced by half.

Turkey Tamales with Red Chili Sauce, Firehouse Chili, and Jicama, Pear, and Watercress Salad.

FIREHOUSE CHILI

2 POUNDS HOT
    ITALIAN SAUSAGE
2½ POUNDS LEAN
    GROUND BEEF
4 CUPS FRESH BEEF
    STOCK (SEE PAGE
    111)
1 TEASPOON
    SAFFRON,
    CRUMBLED
3 TABLESPOONS
    OLIVE OIL
1 CUP CHOPPED
    SHALLOTS
¼ CUP MINCED
    FRESH GARLIC
1½ CUPS DICED
    CANNED GREEN
    CHILIES

Skin and crumble the Italian sausage. Place it in a heavy sauté pan with the ground beef and cook for 15 minutes, or until the meat is brown. Transfer it to a heavy casserole.

Pour the stock into the sauté pan and bring it to a boil. Add the saffron and remove from the heat.

Place the olive oil in a sauté pan over medium heat. Add the shallots and garlic and sauté for 5 minutes, stirring frequently. Remove the mixture from the heat and stir in the chilies, oregano, cumin, cayenne, chili powder, and salt and pepper to taste. Add the tomato paste and half of the stock. Stir to combine, and pour the sauce over the meat. Add the remaining stock and bring to a boil over high heat. Lower the heat and simmer for 1 hour, or until the meat is done and the flavors are well blended.

Add the beans 10 minutes before completion. Serve hot.

1 TEASPOON
    GROUND DRIED
    OREGANO
1½ TEASPOONS
    GROUND CUMIN
¼ TEASPOON
    CAYENNE PEPPER
3 TABLESPOONS
    DARK HOT CHILI
    POWDER
SALT AND PEPPER
    TO TASTE
1 CUP TOMATO
    PASTE
4 CUPS COOKED RED
    KIDNEY BEANS

SERVES 12

JICAMA, PEAR AND WATERCRESS SALAD

1/3 CUP FRESH LIME JUICE
2/3 CUP CORN OIL
PINCH SUGAR
SALT AND PEPPER TO TASTE
3 TABLESPOONS CHOPPED FRESH CORIANDER (CILANTRO)

1 MEDIUM RED ONION
1 BUNCH WATERCRESS
2 POUNDS JICAMA
6 COMICE PEARS

SERVES 12

Whisk together the lime juice, corn oil, sugar, and salt and pepper. When well blended, stir in the chopped coriander and set aside.

Slice the red onion paper thin and set it aside. Wash and trim the stems from the watercress. Dry them thoroughly. Peel the jicama and slice it into a fine julienne. Peel, core, and slice the pears.

Place equal portions of the watercress on each serving plate. Garnish them with julienned jicama and sliced pear. Place red onion slices on top and drizzle the vinaigrette over all.

FUDGE PIE

2 LARGE EGGS
1 CUP SUGAR
1/4 CUP ALL-PURPOSE FLOUR
2 1-OUNCE SQUARES UNSWEETENED CHOCOLATE

1/2 CUP BUTTER
1 UNBAKED 8-INCH PIE SHELL (SEE PAGE 29)

SERVES 8 TO 12

Preheat the oven to 350°.

Beat the eggs and sugar together. Add the flour and beat until blended.

In the top half of a double boiler over boiling water, melt the chocolate and butter. Add it to the flour mixture and beat well.

Pour the filling into the pie shell and bake for 25 minutes, or until the edges are done and the center is set. Allow to cool to room temperature before serving.

Diners are forever.

A Tented Spring Wedding

CREAM OF LETTUCE AND PEA SOUP

NOISETTES OF LAMB WITH VERBENA
AND PIGNOLI

POTATO NAPOLEONS

ROSE SABAYON

SPECIALTY WEDDING CAKE

Wisteria branches gently cascaded from the center poles, baskets overflowed with garden flowers, and chintz and lace draped the tables—these were the finishing touches for the wedding tent. This glamorous wedding in a tent attached to the house fulfilled the bride and groom's every dream.

For both bride and groom, a home extends beyond the house into its surroundings—here a field overlooking the pond. Their Victorian tableware seemed as well placed inside the tent as in the house. The classic menu capped by a breathtaking multi-tiered wedding cake (prepared by a special baker) intensified the nostalgic, dreamlike mood, while the sun's rays obligingly crept across the lawn as afternoon spilled into evening.

Celebrated in a spring garden, the wedding was filled with romantic suggestions of a yet-to-be discovered life together and allowed the guests to share the couple's dreams.

A romantic beginning.

Cream of Lettuce and Pea Soup.

CREAM OF LETTUCE AND PEA SOUP

The welcoming cast iron dogs participate in the day's celebration.

Peel the potatoes and onions and cut into chunks. Place them in a heavy saucepan over medium heat with the Chicken Stock. Cook for about 10 minutes or until the potatoes are tender.

Remove any of the damaged leaves from the lettuce. Core and cut the heads of lettuce into chunks. Add the lettuce, peas, and half of the chives to the potatoes and continue cooking, over low heat, for about 3 more minutes or until the lettuce is just tender but still green. Remove the saucepan from the heat and cool.

When cool, stir in the half-and-half, lemon juice, and salt and pepper to taste.

Purée the soup in a blender or food processor using the metal blade. When smooth, pour into a bowl and refrigerate, covered, for at least 1 hour. When ready to serve, adjust the seasonings. Pour it into soup bowls and garnish with a thin slice of lemon and chopped chives.

1 POUND IDAHO POTATOES

1 POUND ONIONS

6 CUPS FRESH CHICKEN STOCK (SEE PAGE 37)

2 HEADS ICEBERG LETTUCE

2 POUNDS FROZEN PETIT PEAS

1 BUNCH CHOPPED FRESH CHIVES

2 CUPS HALF-AND-HALF

½ CUP FRESH LEMON JUICE

SALT AND PEPPER TO TASTE

12 LEMON SLICES

SERVES 12

NOISETTES OF LAMB WITH VERBENA AND PIGNOLI

Trim the loins, keeping them in one piece. Save the trimmings. In a heavy sauté pan, brown the lamb trimmings in 1 tablespoon of butter. When brown, discard the butter and lamb grease. Add 3½ cups of the Veal Stock, verbena, and fennel seeds. Cook for 20 minutes, stirring occasionally, or until the liquid is reduced by half. When reduced, strain it through a fine sieve. Add the garlic and parsley and set aside.

Slice the loins into 12 ½-inch noisettes.

Melt ¼ cup of the butter in a heavy sauté pan over medium heat. Quickly sear the noisettes for about 1 minute per side to brown and seal in juices. When the noisettes are cooked, deglaze the pan with the remaining Veal Stock and add the deglazing liquid to the verbena essence. Whisk in the remaining butter and stir in the pignoli nuts. To serve, brush the noisettes with sauce and serve the remaining sauce on the side.

2 LOINS OF LAMB

¾ CUP OF UNSALTED BUTTER

4½ CUPS VEAL STOCK

4 TABLESPOONS DRIED VERBENA

1 TEASPOON FENNEL SEED

1 TABLESPOON MINCED FRESH GARLIC

2 TABLESPOONS CHOPPED FRESH ITALIAN PARSLEY

¼ CUP PIGNOLI NUTS

SERVES 12

VEAL STOCK

Follow the recipe for Beef Stock (see page 111) but substitute veal bones for beef, and use white wine instead of red wine. Eliminate the tomatoes.

MAKES 1 QUART

Noisettes of lamb are enhanced by verbena.

POTATO NAPOLEONS

¼ POUND SLAB
  BACON
1 ¼ CUPS UNSALTED
  BUTTER
5 POUNDS IDAHO
  POTATOES
3 CUPS HEAVY
  CREAM
SALT AND PEPPER
  TO TASTE
⅓ CUP CHOPPED
  FRESH CHIVES

SERVES 12

Cut the bacon into ¼-inch cubes. Place in a medium sauté pan over medium heat and cook for about 7 minutes or until they are crisp and brown. Drain the bacon cubes on paper towels and set them aside.

Melt the butter over very low heat in a heavy saucepan. Skim off the white solids and reserve them. Ladle off the clarified butter and set it aside.

Peel the potatoes. On a mandolin, slice 2 potatoes paper thin, or slice into fine juliennes, using the ultra thin slicing disc of a food processor. Immediately put the potato slices in ice water.

Cube the remaining potatoes and place them in a heavy saucepan. Cover them with water, add salt to taste and cook, over medium heat, for about 25 minutes or until tender. Drain the potatoes and place them in the bowl of an electric mixer. Beat until whipped, adding the cream, reserved butter solids, and salt and pepper to taste. If the potatoes are stiff, slowly add up to ¼ cup more of the cream. Fold in the bacon and 2 tablespoons of the chopped chives. Cover and keep them warm.

Drain the potato slices and pat dry. Put the clarified butter in a 10-inch sauté pan and fry the potato slices in batches over medium heat, turning frequently, for about 3 minutes or until lightly browned. Remove them from the heat and place on a baking sheet. Sprinkle them with salt.

To serve, put a dollop of mashed potatoes on each serving plate and top each with a crisp potato slice. Make 2 more layers, ending with a potato slice. Garnish with chopped chives.

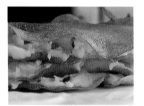

A virtuoso blend of two familiar potato favorites.

134

ROSE SABAYON

The wedding tent.

Combine the orange juice, brown sugar, rose hips, wine, gelatin, and rose water in a medium saucepan. Bring to a slow boil over medium heat, stirring constantly. Cook for about 10 minutes or until the gelatin is dissolved. Strain into a small bowl. Set the bowl in a large bowl filled with ice cubes and whisk the mixture frequently for 5 minutes or until it has cooled and slightly thickened. Set it aside.

Whip the cream until stiff. Fold it into the orange mixture. Tap the bowl lightly on a counter to remove the air bubbles. Cover it with plastic wrap and refrigerate at least 8 hours. When it is well chilled, portion the sabayon by holding 2 tablespoons together as a scoop or use a tiny ice cream scoop. Place 2 portions on each chilled serving plate and garnish them with fresh mint leaves.

1 CUP FRESH ORANGE JUICE
1 CUP DARK BROWN SUGAR
2 TABLESPOONS DRIED ROSE HIPS (AVAILABLE IN MOST HEALTH FOOD STORES)
1½ TEASPOONS WHITE WINE
3 TEASPOONS UNFLAVORED GELATIN
¼ CUP ROSE WATER
4 CUPS HEAVY CREAM
FRESH MINT LEAVES

SERVES 12

A shaded corner.

WAYS
and
MEANS

BUDGETS ARE A REALITY. BUT KEEPING COSTS IN CHECK DOES NOT MEAN SACRIFICING CONCEPT or quality. If you know how to plan and shop well, you can still achieve your individual preferences. And if you cannot accomplish this yourself, consider hiring a professional.

Before you plan a party, commit some time to investigating the costs of food, decor, space, and music. Unless you understand the basic cost of goods, you will not have a yardstick by which you can compare prices. Don't embark on a project unless you have the energy and can afford to carry it out. Set your budget, and then be creative about how to make that budget fulfill your dream.

Operate like a business; be honest about your bottom line. What does it include? Have you left room for changes or hidden costs? Be flexible, in both concept and budget. To stay within your parameters, you may have to revise your concept. If you are at your limit, adjust the style of entertaining or the number of guests.

Food costs generally do not decrease as the number of guests increases, although some items may be less costly per person when purchased in bulk. Remember that a party space that can accommodate two hundred guests will be less expensive per guest for two hundred than for fifty. If you plan to have seating for all guests, serving buffet style will be more expensive than a seated dinner, because more equipment and personnel will be required.

Creative menu planning, budget, and attentive service set the stage.

Complicated aspects of an event require careful budgeting of a host's time.

Consider these items as you finalize your budget for a successful event:

Space: Where is the event to be held? Will it have to be rented? How much for how long? Are there extra charges attached, such as guards, sound equipment, special parking?

Menu: What type of food and how much? How should it be presented?

Equipment: What implements will be needed to prepare and serve the food? Do these have to be rented? Are tables and chairs necessary? Table linens?

Service staff: Will a caterer be used? Do you need bartenders? Waiters? Kitchen staff? Car parks? Coat checks?

Bar: Who will provide this? How much? How many types of liquor? Will you serve wines with dinner? How many?

Invitations: How will your guests be invited? By telephone? With engraved or printed invitations?

Flowers and decor: Where will the flowers be placed? How many arrangements are necessary? Will other decorations be needed, such as sets and stage props?

Music: Will it be for background or for dancing? Taped or live? How much equipment? How many people? How will they be paid?

Lighting: Should professional equipment be brought in? Can anything on location be used?

Entertainment: Special performers?

Party favors: Are mementos necessary?

Parking: Do you want to provide this or have the guests handle it themselves?

Gratuities: Who will expect tips?

Budgeting a private party is solely in the hands of the host. Corporate entertainment budgets are generally established through the office of the company's chief executives. It falls to the corporate executive in charge of special events and the hired professional to find the most creative use of these inflexible funds. For public events, the expense is always determined by the financial goal to be achieved. When working within a set budget, always inform the professionals assisting you of its limitations. This will inspire either more ingenuity or a reconsideration of the event. Insist that suppliers provide you with estimates as close to the final cost as possible.

Suit the budget to company needs. If you have a client roster of a hundred and want to get to know each guest personally, then give ten parties of ten. If, however, you are introducing a new product, entertain everyone at once.

For a public event, first decide what proportion of the ticket price will benefit the charity and how much will be spent on direct costs for the event. Knowing the cost of past events will help you make a decision. Find out where you might be able to rely on underwriting or direct contributions. Learn your guests' financial limits. Discover what guests as well as suppliers expect in return for their support. Carefully do your homework before embarking on the final plans.

Within the past ten years, attendance at major charity functions has increased enormously and will likely continue to grow as governmental funding decreases. As a result, "event budgets" must take on larger expenses, and compensation to suppliers needs to be rethought. When asking for donations of goods and services for fifty, you can anticipate quite a different reaction than when asking for donations for a thousand guests.

The greatest mistake any committee chairperson can make is to assume that suppliers will underwrite an event either by discount or direct contribution. While such discounts and contributions do happen, they cannot be the basis for the economics of fundraising. Seek benefactors who would be flattered to support your organization.

The old adage "you get what you pay for" makes great sense at a fund-raiser, where your treatment of your benefactors will directly respond to their

For parties of any size, service must always operate with military precision.

generosity. Remember that as each year's financial goals expand, so will the need for funds. Do not short-change your benefactors by cutting corners. All professional party planners and caterers will take into consideration the charitable nature of the event and make adjustments, or they will pledge a specific amount to the charity as a corporate benefactor if they charge their regular fee.

If you have been realistic about your budget, an experienced party planner can be innovative within the framework you have set. If you are working on your own, you must learn to cut corners where it won't show. In every case, target your audience and know what you can give and what they expect from you. The earlier you set your plan (six months to a year in advance), send out your invitations (four to six weeks in advance), and organize your costs (throughout the planning stage), the more likely you will be able to keep expenses to a minimum.

Frequently, the theme of your party will dictate the menu; just as often, it does not. Whatever your intention, the most important rule of food service is covered in one word: excellence. Whether you or a caterer prepare the feast, everything must be of the highest quality and in perfect taste. Menus should be well-prepared and have eye-appeal. Think in terms of color and texture. Have only one featured item; if you prepare all of your specialties at one sitting, none will be remembered. Balance and orchestrate flavors carefully. Don't attempt new or untried recipes unless you are positive of their success. Perfectly prepared, foods will never fail to impress your guests.

Whether for a large gathering or a dinner for two, if you choose to do the preparation, plan the menu with an eye to advance cooking, baking, or freezing and ease of service. If you use a caterer, consider his reputation and performance skill and work with him on every detail. In either case, create a menu that is beautiful to look at, easy to digest, pleasant to serve, unexpected, and delicious.

Seated dinners demand care for and interest in the comfort of the individual guest. Seating arrangements should be made with conviviality in mind. Good talk should prevail. If you are serving after-dinner liqueurs, do so in a refreshed setting, not at the dinner table. Keep tables clear, ash trays clean, linen fresh, and glasses full.

Dinner, done with style, is the consummate way to establish a business relationship, build a career, or get to know a new friend. Many a Chateaubriand and burgundy have been served in candlelit corners to inspire a romance. Simplicity is the key word when dining *à deux*. Food, wine, and decor should be unassuming, liquor kept to a festive minimum, lighting and seating conducive to calm words and quiet laughter, and food ready to serve and easy to handle.

When dining outdoors, try prepacked individual lunches or dinners to save last-minute hassle. Public places often allow for easy serving and clean-up and frequently have professional kitchens that can be used for large, catered events. Many cuisines lend themselves to a barbeque or beach cook-out for family or for a business party that will include the employees' families.

Meals are eaten from beginning to end, but they are best planned from the center. Choose your entrée first, then its accompanying vegetables. Next choose appetizer, salad (if there will be one), and then dessert. When the menu is complete, select hors d'oeuvres, if desired. Hors d'oeuvres should be carefully considered: They can excite the palate for what is to follow, or spoil the appetite. "Hors d'oeuvre" means literally "outside the main body of work"; never overplay them before dinner.

Think of a meal as an artwork in its own right, in which taste, shape, color, texture, form, temperature, and aroma interact to create a dramatic whole. Like all works of art, the meal should fascinate or even surprise, and introduce something new. In creating menus, think about the significance of each meal and let that influence your choices. Dinner, no matter when we eat it, is seen as the primary meal of the day. Lunch (for Americans) is seen as a pleasant refresher between breakfast and dinner. Breakfast is purely utilitarian, except on weekends, when it might be converted into brunch. Suppers always seem to be light palate pleasers, with more emphasis on flavor than substance.

A dinner that consists of meat, poultry, or fish; potatoes, rice, or pasta; and vegetables is standard for most Americans. It is, however, only one possible style of serving. Be bold enough to attempt other cultural approaches—one-dish entrées of meat or pasta or platters of mixed vegetables.

Consider serving a salad after the entrée because it will mediate between the preceding strong flavors and the cool temperature of the dessert to follow. Learn to select perfect and delicious individual dishes. However, remember that a meal full of highlights dulls the sensitivity of the taste buds. Plan on breaks of flavor. Look at complete menus in cookbooks, but trust your own instincts enough to recombine things to suit your taste. If you're serving outstanding wines, downplay the flavors of the food so that the wine will be fully savored.

Think of a meal as an artwork in its own right: TOP *A Tuscan Grill.*
BELOW *Japanese confections among the cherry blossoms.*

A tea can be adapted to fit any budget with a little imagination.

Here are some guidelines about what to serve at various types of meals:

Informal luncheons should consist of two courses: a plated entrée and its vegetables, and dessert.

Formal luncheons can consist of three to five courses, including soup, fish, meat and vegetables, salad, and dessert. The preferred choice among Americans is three, omitting the fish and salad.

Informal dinners consist of three courses: appetizer or soup, entrée, and dessert, relying mainly on hors d'oeuvres.

Formal dinners consist of four to six courses: appetizer or soup, fish, entrée, salad, cheese, and dessert. They are usually preceded by very few hors d'oeuvres, but often followed by small baked items. Suppers follow the same format but are lighter.

Buffets usually consist of a choice of two or three entrées, and four or five accompanying vegetables. They are generally preceded by more substantial hors d'oeuvres to take the place of appetizers.

Cocktail receptions are events between meals and should not emphasize food. They are intended to stimulate appetite, so small quantities of a large variety of items are required. Five to nine different hors d'oeuvres are usually enough. Currently the cocktail buffet, or extended cocktail party, has taken the place once occupied by the tea. At such receptions, hors d'oeuvres of more variety and substance are passed—up to twelve separate items. A buffet of additional (usually hot) hors d'oeuvres or a carving station further complement the passed items.

Brunch usually consists of a one-plate meal, either served or self-served, preceded by light cocktails and completed with coffee and dessert.

Teas consist of an array of bite-size or small-plate-size savories and sweets, limited only by budget and imagination. Of the savories, the tea sandwich is the highlight.

Picnics run the full gamut of all other meals, and their components are determined by the place, time of year, and time of day. In planning the menu, remember that picnic food usually must travel and be stored without temperature control. On the whole, most picnics are informal and the menu selection follows suit. However, a formal picnic may be an exciting twist to menu planning.

Learn to be flexible enough to accommodate different tastes and eating styles. Consider including a vegetarian menu for guests with those requirements, and be sure the meal is prepared with as much attention as that of your other guests. Don't just "double up" on the vegetables. Likewise, if you have guests who eat kosher, consult a kosher caterer or supplier who meets your standards.

Always anticipate the unexpected. Plan on more food than you think you will need. Be prepared, unless you're planning a formal dinner, to offer second portions if guests request them. Have herbal teas and decaffeinated coffee available.

When you are involved in corporate entertaining on an intimate scale, let the preferences of the corporate host dictate the menu. If entertaining unfamiliar corporate clients, diplomats, or government officials, contact their offices to find out if they have any dietary restrictions or allergies, or particular likes or dislikes.

When planning the menu for a public event, remember that the greater the attendance, the more familiar food choices should be. A well-prepared classic is appreciated more than something unknown. Create a menu to reflect the generosity and style of your benefactors. Use items that are considered extravagant lavishly or don't use them at all. The food should be consistent and the courses should not compete. Ask your caterer for a tasting and adjust your choices. Choose foods that allow for changes in the schedule, such as holding dinner until the guest speaker is ready to begin. Since most public spaces do not come equipped with full kitchens, depend on the judgment of your caterer to suggest a successful menu.

At formal dinners, place one menu card between two place settings so guests know what to expect. Use the back of the card to acknowledge contributions and suppliers.

If you plan to have a bar, place it in a spot accessible to all guests at all times. Whenever possible, it is best to have drinks served from a service bar located somewhere out of sight.

Although most bartenders will mix appropriately balanced cocktails, take the precaution of asking the bartender to mix by measure, not by eye.

Here is our suggested bar stock for a cocktail party for fifty to seventy-five guests:

1 small white vermouth, dry
1 small red vermouth, sweet
3 liters gin
1 liter bourbon
4 liters vodka
4 liters scotch
6 fifths red wine
1 case white wine
2 liters Canadian whiskey
1 liter rum

No matter what the occasion, choose your wines carefully and serve them at the correct temperature. If your knowledge of correctly combining wine with food is weak, defer to a professional. As you learn to evaluate wines, examine the following properties:

Appearance: a filled glass held against a white napkin should have good color. Wines under five years old should not be murky or "off" in color.
Bouquet: aroma should be fresh and clean, reflecting the grape's taste.
Taste: should be clean, without bitterness or acidity.
Aftertaste: if too heavy, this indicates acidity.

A good wine glass should hold at least eight ounces, so that you can swirl the wine and open the bouquet. Don't fill the glass more than one-third full. Let a full-bodied red wine breathe for fifteen minutes; a full-bodied but immature red wine for a half hour to an hour; a rosé or ordinary red wine for just five minutes.

Make your wine selection with the same dramatic force as you did the menu. Match a mature vintage with the entrée, preceded by a younger, lesser wine of the same type. This young wine prepares the nose and palate for the forthcoming luxurious flavor. Do not serve wines with salads or other courses that are strongly dependent on a vinaigrette dressing. Dessert wines and champagne deserve a food-free space at the end of the meal to be enjoyed on their own.

When serving wine, temperature is of the utmost importance. A superb wine can be ruined by over-chilling it or allowing it to get too warm. Serve champagne cold and keep it cold. Serve white wines cool, except white burgundies, which should be served at near room temperature. Almost all red wines should be served at room temperature but kept away from heat. Some reds, like Beaujolais, are best served cool, and dessert wines are always served cool.

In estimating your wine needs, plan on each guest having two five-ounce glasses of each wine you are serving. Calculate that each bottle will serve two to three guests, and therefore each case will serve thirty-six guests, or approximately seventy-two glasses. If your menu calls for more than two wines, estimate that your guests will drink only one glass of each wine, with the exception of the wine served with the entrée course.

Although most oenophiles would disagree, we believe that wines are to be tasted and enjoyed and not discussed too much. If you are inexperienced with wines, seek opportunities to taste new ones. Save labels from those that you like and note the reasons why. Trust your palate, and if something tastes acidic or fruity to you, note it. You may be able to define what that means at a later date.

In all situations where service is required, you should, as host, delineate your expectations. This can be done directly to the server, maître d' or captain. The maître d' or supervisor is the most important person in service to you. He or she will represent your wishes during the event. Explain politely and firmly what you want. Then let them do what they do best—execute a successful party.

In selecting a service style, you will have to decide between three basic types: French Service, whereby the entrée is served from a tray by the waiter to the guest using a serving fork and spoon; American Service, whereby plates are made up in the kitchen by the chef and his staff and presented to the guests; and Russian Service, whereby the waiter presents the tray to the guest and the guest serves his own plate. French Service is the preferred type for large groups; it guarantees speedy service at the correct temperature.

The well-trained waiter should know the difference between good and poor service, between show and bluff. His manner is neither servile nor arrogant, but courteous. He should be knowledgeable about American, French, and Russian styles as well as wine and beverage service. While no one manner of table service is the only correct one, the waiter should know which would better meet the needs of the guests and the situation as explained by the host. The waiter should also prepare the dining area or party area. Besides serving the food, he should set up and take down all necessary equipment.

Good service keeps the movement of a party flowing. Dishes are cleared two at a time, never stacked. Always serve counterclockwise, beginning with the guest of honor. Serve from the left, remove from the right, and pour liquids from the right. Service people should stimulate mingling during cocktails by passing drinks and hors d'oeuvres among the guests. During seated dinners, service should never be intrusive. It should be quiet, fast, and direct.

If you are serving with no help, follow these guidelines:

1. Keep menus simple, preceded by plenty of substantial hors d'oeuvres that have been placed in the room before guests arrive.

2. Consider setting up food on a sideboard and having guests serve themselves.

3. If possible, serve a room-temperature meal.

4. Guests should never help you clear away dishes and never feel pressed into joining you in the clean-up afterwards. Considerate guests will not insist too much.

Set your budget, know your style. Get help when you need it. Keep your goal in mind at all times, and you will find the best way to entertain successfully within your budget.

A Victorian Tea

MINIATURE CORNISH BEEF PASTIES

CHEDDAR ROUNDS

TEA SANDWICHES

SCONES

COCONUT LEMON SQUARES

YORKSHIRE FAT RASCALS

ECCLES CAKES

RICHMOND MAIDS OF HONOR

DUNDEE CAKE

WALNUT CAKE

MINIATURE MINCEMEAT POCKETS

TRIFLE

FLUMMERY

A SAMPLER OF TEAS

When the Victorian Society asked us to help raise scholarship funds for students of nineteenth-century architecture, culture, and decorative arts, we created an afternoon tea buffet in an elegant Victorian style. Center stage at Carnegie Hall, we laid out a long buffet table resplendent with sterling silver tea sets filled with aromatic teas, baskets of bite-size delectables, and lovely Wedgwood and majolica china. In keeping with Victorian taste, which considered furniture legs too suggestive for public gatherings, the tables were draped with chintz and lace tablecloths that fell to the floor. A sense of opulence—encouraged by lavish bouquets and copious dishes—and a playful emphasis on decorum set the mood for our Victorian gala.

The floral abundance of spring is coupled with Victorian excess.

A party that transports guests to another era is a welcome escape from the day-to-day world of practical concerns. Strict authenticity is hardly necessary: The goal is to create a rich sense of the period. The guests at our Victorian tea became players in a drama, giving them pleasure, as well as heightening their enthusiasm to help fund the study of this remarkable period.

MINIATURE CORNISH BEEF PASTIES

TART DOUGH (SEE PAGE 29)
1 TEASPOON DIJON MUSTARD
½ POUND LEAN GROUND BEEF
1 STRIP BACON, FINELY GROUND
1 TABLESPOON CATSUP
1 TABLESPOON GRATED ONION
1 TABLESPOON CHOPPED FRESH ITALIAN PARSLEY
1 TEASPOON MINCED GARLIC

1 TABLESPOON WORCESTERSHIRE SAUCE
PINCH EACH OF GROUND MACE, THYME, CLOVE, BAY LEAF
SALT AND PEPPER TO TASTE
1 LARGE EGG
2 TABLESPOONS MILK

SERVES 12

Preheat the oven to 375°.

Roll out the dough to ⅛-inch thick and cut it into 4-inch circles. Brush each circle with mustard.

Combine the ground beef, bacon, catsup, onion, parsley, garlic, Worcestershire sauce, herbs, and salt and pepper to taste until well blended.

Whisk the egg and milk until well combined.

Place approximately 1 tablespoon of the beef mixture in the center of each dough circle and fold it over in half. Seal the edges with a fork and brush the top with the egg wash.

Place the pasties on a greased cookie sheet and bake them for 15 to 20 minutes, or until light brown. Serve warm.

CHEDDAR ROUNDS

½ CUP GRATED EXTRA SHARP CHEDDAR
¼ CUP SALTED BUTTER
DASH TABASCO SAUCE
⅛ TEASPOON CAYENNE PEPPER
¾ CUP ALL-PURPOSE FLOUR
24 SPANISH OLIVES, PITTED

SERVES 12

Preheat the oven to 400°.

In a food processor, using the metal blade, combine the cheese, butter, Tabasco, and cayenne pepper until well blended. Gradually add the flour, mixing until the dough pulls away from the sides of the bowl.

Take a walnut-sized piece of dough and wrap it around a Spanish olive to form a ball.

Place the balls on an ungreased cookie sheet and bake for about 10 minutes, or until lightly browned.

Remove them from the heat and cool on a wire rack. Serve at room temperature.

Tea Sandwiches

The tea sandwich, a most delicate finger food, is traditionally filled with watercress, radish, chicken, or cucumber. But we have found that novel fillings such as potted shrimp, paper-thin roast veal, marinated artichoke bottoms, and smoked duck add a contemporary sparkle.

Whatever filling you choose, here are some guidelines that should be followed for authentic preparation:

The bread should be fresh, thinly sliced, and with trimmed crusts. The filling is sliced or spread thinner than the thickness of the bread. Before the filling is added, the bread should be spread with butter or mayonnaise.

Always place ready-made sandwiches on damp (not wet) tea towels and cover them with more damp towels until ready to serve.

You may wish to use cookie cutters to shape interesting sandwiches. However, since a Victorian tea is a formal affair, avoid cute cutters. Keep the designs simple.

Try spreading butter or mayonnaise on the edges of the sandwiches and then dipping them in fresh chopped herbs, cracked pepper, paprika, grated cheese, or any combination of these. Arrange sandwiches carefully on silver platters lined with lace napkins or doilies, and garnish them with greenery, fresh flowers, or carved vegetables.

An array of tea sandwiches.

SCONES

2 CUPS ALL-
PURPOSE FLOUR
2 TABLESPOONS
SUGAR
1 TABLESPOON
BAKING POWDER
⅓ CUP CHILLED
UNSALTED
BUTTER
1 LARGE EGG YOLK
½ CUP HEAVY CREAM
¼ CUP CURRANTS

SERVES 12

Preheat the oven to 425°.

In a food processor, using the metal blade, combine the flour, sugar, and baking powder. Add the chilled butter and process the mixture to the consistency of coarse meal.

Whisk together the egg yolk and cream and gradually add it to the flour mixture until the dough pulls away from the sides of the bowl. Not all the cream will be used.

Remove the dough from the processor bowl and mix in the currants by hand.

Roll the dough out on a lightly floured board to ¾-inch thick and cut it into 3-inch circles. Place them on a buttered baking sheet and brush them with the remaining heavy cream. Bake 10 minutes, or until golden brown. Serve warm.

COCONUT LEMON SQUARES

1 CUP ALL-PURPOSE
FLOUR
½ CUP UNSALTED
BUTTER
½ CUP
CONFECTIONERS'
SUGAR
2 LARGE EGGS
1 CUP GRANULATED
SUGAR
½ TEASPOON BAKING
POWDER

1 TABLESPOON
FRESH LEMON
JUICE
2 TEASPOONS
GRATED FRESH
LEMON RIND
½ CUP SHREDDED
COCONUT

SERVES 12

Preheat the oven to 350°.

In a food processor, using the metal blade, combine the flour, butter, and confectioners' sugar to form a stiff dough.

Line a 6 x 10-inch ungreased baking sheet with the dough. Prick it all over with a fork and bake for 15 minutes, or until set.

Beat together the eggs, sugar, baking powder, lemon juice, and lemon rind until light and fluffy. Stir in the coconut. When well blended, pour the mixture into the warm crust and spread it to cover.

Bake the squares for 20 minutes, or until just firm. Remove the pan from the heat and cool it on a wire rack. Cut the cookies into 1½-inch squares to serve.

YORKSHIRE FAT RASCALS

3 CUPS ALL-
PURPOSE FLOUR
⅔ CUP SUGAR
½ TEASPOON BAKING
POWDER
⅛ TEASPOON
GROUND NUTMEG
2 TEASPOONS
GRATED FRESH
LEMON RIND

1 CUP CHILLED
UNSALTED
BUTTER
1 LARGE EGG,
BEATEN
¾ CUP CURRANTS

SERVES 12

Preheat the oven to 400°.

In a food processor, using the metal blade, combine the flour, ½ cup of the sugar, the baking powder, nutmeg, and lemon rind. Add the butter and process to cut it in. Add the egg and process to form a stiff dough. Mix in the currants by hand.

Roll the dough out on a lightly floured board to ½-inch thick. Cut the dough into 2-inch circles and sprinkle them with the remaining sugar.

Place them on a greased cookie sheet and bake for 15 minutes, or until just lightly browned. Cool the cookies on a wire rack.

Eccles Cakes

Preheat the oven to 400°.

Begin to melt the butter in a heavy saucepan over low heat. When it is slightly melted, add the dark brown sugar, spices, and currants. Stir until the butter is completely melted and the ingredients are well combined. Remove from the heat and stir in the apple.

Roll out the pastry on a lightly floured board to ¼-inch thick and cut out 3-inch circles. Fill each circle with 1 teaspoon of the apple filling. Moisten the edges of the circles with some of the milk and fold each circle in half. Seal the edges and flatten the cakes slightly. Make 3 parallel slits in the tops, brush them with milk, and sprinkle them with some of the granulated sugar.

Place the cakes on a baking sheet and bake for 12 minutes, or until browned. Remove them from the heat and sprinkle them with the remaining granulated sugar. Serve warm.

¼ UNSALTED BUTTER
3 TABLESPOONS DARK BROWN SUGAR
½ TEASPOON ALLSPICE
¼ TEASPOON GROUND NUTMEG
½ CUP CURRANTS
1 RED DELICIOUS APPLE, PEELED, CORED, AND GRATED
PUFF PASTRY
¼ CUP MILK
¼ CUP GRANULATED SUGAR

SERVES 12

PUFF PASTRY

In a food processor, using the metal blade, cut ¼ cup of the chilled butter into the flour. When well incorporated, add the water and lemon juice, with the motor running, until the dough forms a ball and is workable.

Roll the dough out on a lightly floured, chilled surface to about 9 x 12-inches. Cut the remaining butter into small pieces and lay it out in the center of the dough. Fold the dough into thirds, the edge nearest you first and the far edge last. Pinch the edges together and roll the dough out to the same size it was before folding. Fold and pinch the edges as before. *Do not allow the butter to break through the dough.*

Wrap the pastry dough in clear plastic wrap and refrigerate it for 30 minutes.

Repeat the rolling, folding, and chilling 6 additional times. After the last chilling, allow at least an additional 30 minutes before handling. Roll and cut as directed in the recipe.

1 CUP UNSALTED BUTTER, CHILLED
2 CUPS ALL-PURPOSE FLOUR
⅓ CUP ICE WATER
1 TEASPOON FRESH LEMON JUICE

Bountiful sweets.

RICHMOND MAIDS OF HONOR

1 LARGE EGG
½ CUP PLUS 1 TABLESPOON SUGAR
1 CUP GROUND ALMONDS
¼ CUP MILK
1 TABLESPOON DARK RUM

GRATED RIND OF 1 LEMON
¼ CUP SLICED ALMONDS
PUFF PASTRY (SEE PAGE 151)

SERVES 12

Preheat the oven to 350°.

Beat the egg, gradually adding the sugar until light and fluffy. Add the ground almonds, milk, rum, and lemon rind and mix until well combined.

Roll out the puff pastry as thinly as possible and cut it into 2½-inch circles. Line ungreased miniature muffin cups with the circles and fill them with the almond mixture. Top each with a few sliced almonds. Bake for 15 minutes, or until golden brown.

DUNDEE CAKE

½ CUP WHITE RAISINS
½ CUP BLACK RAISINS
½ CUP CURRANTS
¼ CUP CANDIED LEMON PEEL
10 WHOLE CANDIED CHERRIES
½ CUP GROUND ALMONDS
1 CUP UNSALTED BUTTER
1 CUP SUGAR

GRATED RIND OF 1 ORANGE
4 LARGE EGGS
2¼ CUPS ALL-PURPOSE FLOUR
1 TEASPOON BAKING POWDER
1 TABLESPOON SHERRY
¼ CUP WHOLE ALMONDS

SERVES 12

Preheat the oven to 350°. Grease and flour an 8 x 3-inch high round cake pan. Set it aside.

Mix the raisins, currants, lemon peel, cherries, and ground almonds until well combined. Set the mixture aside.

Cream the butter and sugar until light and fluffy. Add the grated orange rind and eggs and beat until well blended.

Sift together the flour and baking powder and gradually add it to the batter. Stir in the sherry and the combined fruits. Pour the batter into the prepared pan and decorate the top with the whole almonds.

Bake for about 2 hours, or until a knife inserted in the center comes out clean. Cool the cake on a wire rack for 10 minutes, then release it from the pan.

WALNUT CAKE

1 CUP ALL-PURPOSE FLOUR
1½ TEASPOONS BAKING SODA
½ TEASPOON GROUND ALLSPICE
⅔ CUP DARK BROWN SUGAR
1 CUP UNSALTED BUTTER
1 TABLESPOON ALMOND PASTE

3 LARGE EGGS, SEPARATED
1 TEASPOON VANILLA EXTRACT
1 CUP SOUR CREAM
¼ CUP GRANULATED SUGAR
1 CUP WALNUT PIECES

SERVES 12

Preheat the oven to 350°. Grease and flour a 9-inch loaf pan and set it aside.

Sift together the flour, baking soda, and allspice. Set aside.

Cream the dark brown sugar, butter, and almond paste until very light. Add the egg yolks, and beat until combined. Stir in the vanilla. Beat in the dry ingredients alternately with the sour cream.

Beat the egg whites with the granulated sugar until stiff and glossy. Fold them into the batter alternately with the walnut pieces.

Pour the batter into the prepared pan and bake for 30 minutes, or until a knife inserted in the center of the cake comes out clean. Cool it on a wire rack.

MINIATURE MINCEMEAT POCKETS

1 LARGE EGG
¼ CUP MILK
PUFF PASTRY (SEE PAGE 151)
1 CUP PREPARED MINCEMEAT
2 TABLESPOONS SUGAR

SERVES 12

Preheat the oven to 350°.

Whisk together the egg and milk and set aside.

Roll 2 sheets of pastry to fit a ravioli cutter. Fill the centers of the bottom layers with the prepared mincemeat. Cover with the second sheet of pastry and complete the ravioli-making process following manufacturer's directions.

When the squares are cut, brush them with the egg wash. Cut 2 small slits in the top of each and sprinkle them with the sugar. Place them on an ungreased baking sheet and bake for 7 minutes, or until golden. Serve warm.

TRIFLE

12 LARGE EGGS
1½ CUPS SUGAR
1 TEASPOON VANILLA EXTRACT
2 CUPS SIFTED ALL-PURPOSE FLOUR
¾ CUP MELTED UNSALTED BUTTER
½ CUP BRANDY
½ CUP SHERRY
1 CUP RASPBERRY JAM
PASTRY CREAM
1½ CUPS WHIPPED CREAM
¼ CUP CANDIED VIOLETS
3 TABLESPOONS TOASTED SLIVERED ALMONDS

SERVES 12

Preheat the oven to 350°. Butter and flour a 9 x 12-inch sheet pan and set it aside.

Place the eggs, sugar, and vanilla in an electric mixer bowl set in several inches of boiling water. Whisk constantly until the mixture is warm. Place the bowl back on the mixer and beat the mixture on high until it triples in volume, becomes pale yellow, and forms a ribbon when the blades are lifted.

Quickly fold the flour into the mixture. *Do not overmix.*

Gently but quickly fold in the melted butter.

Pour the batter into the prepared pan and bake for 20 minutes, or until the cake has moved away from the sides of the pan.

Allow to cool for 5 minutes. Continue cooling on a wire rack.

Cut the cooled cake into rounds to fit a deep trifle (or soufflé) bowl, piecing together cake when necessary. Place a complete cake round into the bottom of the bowl. Sprinkle it with brandy and sherry and coat it with raspberry jam.

Pour on enough Pastry Cream to make a ½-inch layer.

Complete another cake layer as above, and add Pastry Cream to cover. Make as many layers as you have cake and Pastry Cream.

Top the trifle with whipped cream and garnish it with candied violets and slivered almonds.

PASTRY CREAM

Bring the milk and vanilla bean to a boil in a heavy saucepan over medium heat.

Blend the flour, cornstarch, sugar, and egg yolks in a heavy saucepan over low heat. Gradually whisk the hot milk into the egg mixture, beating rapidly and constantly until the cream is quite thick. Remove the cream from the heat and stir occasionally until it cools.

4 CUPS MILK
1 1-INCH PIECE VANILLA BEAN
⅔ CUP ALL-PURPOSE FLOUR
2 TEASPOONS CORNSTARCH
1 CUP SUGAR
8 LARGE EGG YOLKS

FLUMMERY

5¼ CUPS HEAVY CREAM
2½ CUPS LIGHT CREAM
¾ CUP SLIVERED ALMONDS
¾ CUP GROUND ALMONDS
1¼ TEASPOON ALMOND EXTRACT

In a heavy saucepan over medium heat, combine the creams, almonds, and extract. Cook, stirring constantly, until the mixture comes to a boil. Immediately remove it from the heat and allow to cool.

Dissolve the gelatin in the boiling water and whisk it into the almond mixture. When well combined, pour the mixture into a charlotte mold that has been dipped into very hot water. Cover and refrigerate it for at least 8 hours.

Just before serving, dip the mold in hot water and immediately turn the flummery out onto a serving dish. Garnish it with fresh fruit or berries and serve immediately.

5 TABLESPOONS UNFLAVORED GELATIN
5 TABLESPOONS BOILING WATER
3 CUPS SLICED OR CUBED MIXED FRESH FRUIT OR BERRIES

SERVES 12

A SAMPLER OF TEAS

The large variety of teas available today presents almost limitless possibilities for a tasting sampler. The selection of sixteen teas presented here are our favorites.

LARGE LEAF TEAS (Brew 5 to 6 minutes)

China Oolong: A gentle brown tea with an exquisite flavor often likened to that of ripe peaches. Try it with fruit, crepes, or tarts.
Earl Grey: A unique blend of China and Darjeeling teas famous for its fragrance and delicate bergamot flavor. Good with seafood or sweet desserts.
Green Gunpowder: Gets its name from the unfermented leaves neatly rolled into pellet-like shapes. The tea is fragrant and very pale with a mild, slightly tart flavor. Excellent with Chinese and Japanese dishes.

Lapsang Souchong: Smoky, elegant, a tea for the cultivated palate. Its pungent flavor comes in part from the mineral-rich soil of China's Fukien province, where it is grown. Try it with highly flavored fish and poultry, such as salmon or duck, or with crisp cucumber sandwiches.

Prince of Wales: A richly colored, mellow tea from the Anhwei province of China. This is a classic blend, considered to be the "Burgundy" of China teas. Good all day long, but try it after dinner with a cheese and fruit dessert.

Russian Caravan: A fragrant blend of fine-quality China black and oolong brown teas. The rich brew was highly cherished by the old Russian aristocracy. Savor it with stroganoff or with pashka, the traditional Russian Easter delicacy.

Vintage Darjeeling: Rarest of teas, a noble slow-growing leaf gathered in the proper season from the highest Himalayan tea gardens. The ultimate brew for afternoon teatime. Sip it with the thinnest of watercress or chicken sandwiches.

Yunnan: A sweetly fragrant, golden tea from the rarest leaves in China's Yunnan province. Try it as a refreshing contrast to Hunan or Szechuan dishes.

Ceylon Breakfast: With its flowery bouquet and light golden liquor, this is the mildest of the breakfast blends. It also makes clear, cloudless iced tea. Try quantities of it iced with Mexican foods.

Lemon-scented: A light, refreshing tea scented and flavored with natural lemon essence. A natural for icing. Serve it by the pitcher next time you cook outdoors.

Orange Pekoe: A brisk, smooth, high-grown Ceylon tea, good for lunch or early afternoon. Also recommended with Persian and other Middle-Eastern cuisines.

Queen Mary: Delicate and refreshing, the personal blend of the late Queen Mary. Serve it for afternoon tea with scones and clotted cream, or with strawberry shortcake in the summer.

Spiced: A rich, aromatic tea mixed with cut cloves and dried orange peel for an exciting flavor. Add rum and a cinnamon stick on a wintry day, or make it the base for a party punch.

SMALL LEAF TEAS (Brew 3 minutes)

English Breakfast: A lively, full-bodied blend of Ceylon and Indian teas, famous as a wake-up brew. Serve it for breakfast with hot muffins or croissants.

Assam: A brisk, full-bodied tea with a distinct malty taste. A hearty eye-opener from the Assam region of northern India. Serve it with a robust steak-and-eggs breakfast. It also stands up to the spiciest Indian dishes.

Irish Breakfast: A robust, pungent, extremely satisfying tea. A hearty accompaniment to traditional English fare like shepherd's pie or Cornish pasties.

NOTE: Tea bags do not need to brew as long as loose tea. They contain broken leaves, designed to release their flavor in just a minute or two after immersion in water.

Chintz, lace, and majolica dress the guest tables.

How to Brew Tea

1. Fill a kettle with fresh, cold water—let it run a bit first. This ensures that the water will be full of oxygen, which brings out tea's best flavor.

2. While the water is heating, put some hot water into the teapot. (Earthenware, porcelain, or glass pots are best; silver is fine for formal occasions; but never use aluminum, which taints the tea.) Swirl the hot water around a little to warm the pot and then pour it out.

3. Add the tea leaves. Use 1 teaspoon of tea for each cup plus 1 teaspoon for the pot, but experiment.

4. As *soon* as the water reaches a full rolling boil, pour it over the tea leaves and cover the pot. Overboiling will let too much oxygen out of the water, and the tea will be flat.

5. Allow the tea to brew about 3 minutes for a small-leaf tea, or 5 to 6 minutes for a large-leaf tea. Stir gently.

6. To serve, pour hot tea through a strainer into a teacup.

7. For a stronger brew, use extra tea. Don't extend the brewing time, since overbrewing releases tannin and makes the tea bitter.

8. If the tea is too strong, add a little hot water. If it's too weak, start over.

A tea service.

A Midsummer Tuscan Feast

PIGNOLI-STUFFED MUSSELS

SUPPLI AL TELEFONO

BISTECCA FIORENTINA

GRILLED QUAILS WITH SAGE

OYSTERS WITH BALSAMIC VINAIGRETTE

BRUSCHETTA

ITALIAN SEAFOOD SALAD

BLOOD ORANGE, ARUGULA, AND MASCARPONE
SALAD

PASTA CAPRESE

EGGPLANT AGRO DOLCE

AMARETTO STUFFED PEARS

PEACHES UNDER BAROLO

A picnic under the noonday sun next to the grape arbor seemed perfect for a big family reunion. Everyone joined in to solve the basic question: "What's for lunch?" The consensus was to choose from among the best of the season, direct from the farmer's market. Searching for superb quality and just-picked freshness became an entertainment itself as young and old joined in the shopping and had a heated discussion about each item on the menu. What a feast resulted—a family reunion that revitalized the old, invigorated the young, and gave peace and serenity to all.

The simple and timeless joys of food fresh from the market.

PIGNOLI-STUFFED MUSSELS

24 MUSSELS, IN SHELLS
2 CUPS WHITE WINE
3 TABLESPOONS OLIVE OIL
¼ CUP MINCED ONIONS
⅓ CUP LONG GRAIN RICE
¼ CUP PIGNOLI NUTS
2 TABLESPOONS CURRANTS
1 CUP CLAM JUICE
SALT AND PEPPER TO TASTE
2 TEASPOONS CHOPPED FRESH ITALIAN PARSLEY

SERVES 12

Soak and scrub the mussels well.

Place the wine and mussels in a steamer pot and steam until the mussels open. Remove the pot from the heat and allow to cool.

Heat the olive oil in a large sauté pan over low heat. Add the onion, rice, and pignoli nuts. Raise the heat and sauté for 3 minutes, or until the pignoli nuts are golden. Immediately add the currants and clam juice. Stir to mix. Add salt and pepper to taste. Cover, raise the heat, and bring the mixture to a boil. Lower the heat and cook for 20 minutes, or until the rice is done and all the liquid is absorbed. (If more liquid is needed, use the wine remaining in the steamer pot.)

Stir in the chopped parsley and remove the pot from the heat. Preheat the oven to 400°.

Open the mussels fully and break off the empty half shells. Cover each mussel with the rice mixture, packing it down firmly. Place the mussels on a baking sheet and bake for 5 minutes, or until the rice mixture is set and lightly browned. Serve the mussels hot or at room temperature.

Pignoli-stuffed Mussels garnished with green and purple basil.

SUPPLI AL TELEFONO

1¼ CUPS FRESH CHICKEN STOCK (SEE PAGE 37)
1 TABLESPOON SALTED BUTTER
2 TABLESPOONS ONION PUREE
⅓ CUP LONG GRAIN RICE
¼ CUP DRY WHITE WINE
SALT TO TASTE
1 LARGE EGG
2 TABLESPOONS GRATED PARMESAN CHEESE
2 OUNCES MOZZARELLA CHEESE
2 CUPS CORN OIL
1 CUP SEASONED ITALIAN BREAD CRUMBS

SERVES 12

In a small saucepan over medium heat, bring the Chicken Stock to a boil. Lower the heat and keep the stock at a simmer.

In another heavy-bottomed saucepan, melt the butter over medium heat. Add the onion purée and cook for 2 minutes, but do not brown. Add the rice and cook, stirring constantly, for 2 minutes, or until the rice glistens. Pour in the wine. Raise the heat and boil for 5 minutes, or until almost all the liquid is absorbed.

Add half of the simmering stock and, stirring constantly, cook for 10 minutes, or until it begins to be absorbed.

Continue adding stock as it is absorbed until all the stock is used. Add salt to taste. The rice should be very thick.

Spread the rice out on a baking sheet. Allow it to cool, then refrigerate it, uncovered, for at least 8 hours to dry out.

Mix the egg and Parmesan cheese. Set aside.

Cut the mozzarella cheese into ½-inch-square cubes. Press the rice around the mozzarella to form 1-inch balls.

Bring the oil to 350° in a deep-sided pot or deep fryer.

Dip the rice balls in the egg mixture, then in the bread crumbs. Immediately drop them into the hot oil, a few at a time, and fry them for 3 minutes, or until golden. Serve hot.

BISTECCA FIORENTINA

12 8-OUNCE SHELL
STEAKS
¾ POUND SALTED
BUTTER,
SOFTENED

Brush each steak with softened butter. Coat them with salt and pepper. Place the steaks on a hot grill and cook them as desired— 3 minutes per side for rare. Serve immediately.

COARSE SALT TO
TASTE
CRACKED PEPPER TO
TASTE

SERVES 12

GRILLED QUAILS WITH SAGE

Grilled Quails with Sage.

Wash and dry the quails.

Place a teaspoonful of sage into each quail cavity. Wrap each quail with 1 slice of bacon and secure with a toothpick.

Mix the olive oil and minced garlic and brush it generously on each quail.

Place the quails on a hot grill and cook for 6 minutes per side, or until done. Let them rest 5 minutes before serving.

12 QUAILS
¼ CUP MINCED
FRESH SAGE
12 SLICES BACON
½ CUP OLIVE OIL
1 TABLESPOON
MINCED FRESH
GARLIC

SERVES 12

OYSTERS WITH BALSAMIC VINAIGRETTE

Scrub the oysters well. Place cleaned oysters on a hot grill, curve side down. As the oysters open, remove them from the grill, holding in as much juice as possible.

While they are still warm, top the oysters with Balsamic Vinaigrette and serve immediately.

36 LARGE FRESH
OYSTERS
BALSAMIC
VINAIGRETTE

SERVES 12

BALSAMIC VINAIGRETTE

½ CUP WHITE WINE
½ CUP BALSAMIC
VINEGAR
¼ CUP MINCED
FRESH SHALLOTS

Combine all the ingredients until well blended. Refrigerate the vinaigrette until ready to use.

2 TABLESPOONS
MINCED FRESH
ITALIAN PARSLEY
1 TABLESPOON
GROUND PEPPER

Brushed with Gorgonzola cheese, slices of toasted peasant bread magically become Bruschetta.

BRUSCHETTA

1 LARGE LOAF
TUSCAN BREAD
(OR ANY OTHER
DENSE, CRUSTY,
PEASANT BREAD)

Slice the bread into ½-inch thick pieces. Place the slices on a hot grill and toast them until light brown on each side.

Immediately brush each slice with whipped Gorgonzola and serve hot.

½ POUND
GORGONZOLA
CHEESE, WHIPPED

SERVES 12

ITALIAN SEAFOOD SALAD

1½ POUNDS SHRIMP,
COOKED, PEELED,
AND DEVEINED

2 POUNDS SQUID,
CLEANED, SLICED,
AND STEAMED

3 POUNDS COOKED
FRESH MUSSELS,
SHELLED

2 POUNDS COOKED
FRESH LOBSTER,
SHELLED

½ CUP FRESH LEMON
JUICE

1½ CUPS EXTRA
VIRGIN OLIVE OIL

Toss all the cooked seafood together in a serving bowl.

Whisk together the lemon juice, olive oil, garlic, herbs, red pepper flakes, and salt and pepper to taste. Pour the dressing over the seafood. Cover and refrigerate for 2 hours, stirring often.

Wash and trim the celery. Cut the stalks on a diagonal into ¼-inch slices. Add them to the seafood and let the salad rest for 15 minutes before serving.

5 TABLESPOONS
MINCED FRESH
GARLIC

½ TEASPOON DRIED
BASIL

½ TEASPOON DRIED
OREGANO

½ TEASPOON DRIED
RED PEPPER
FLAKES

SALT AND PEPPER
TO TASTE

1 BUNCH CELERY

SERVES 12

Blood oranges and arugula, dotted with Mascarpone cheese.

BLOOD ORANGE, ARUGULA, AND MASCARPONE SALAD

4 BLOOD ORANGES
3 BUNCHES ARUGULA
3 LARGE RED ONIONS
½ CUP EXTRA VIRGIN OLIVE OIL
3 TABLESPOONS SHERRY WINE VINEGAR
1 TABLESPOON SUGAR

SALT AND PEPPER TO TASTE
1 POUND MASCARPONE CHEESE
1 CUP TOASTED PIGNOLI NUTS

SERVES 12

Peel and slice the oranges crosswise, making 6 slices per orange. Set aside.

Wash, trim, and dry the arugula.

Peel and slice the onions, crosswise, making 8 slices per onion.

Whisk together the olive oil, vinegar, sugar, and salt and pepper.

Place the arugula on a serving platter. Arrange alternating slices of orange and onion around the edges of the arugula. Place small ice-cream scoops of Mascarpone cheese at intervals on the oranges and onions. Sprinkle all with the pignoli nuts.

Drizzle the vinaigrette over all and serve.

PASTA CAPRESE

1½ POUNDS UNCOOKED PENNE
1 CUP OLIVE OIL
1 POUND MOZZARELLA CHEESE, JULIENNED
1 POUND PLUM TOMATOES, PEELED, SEEDED, AND JULIENNED

1½ CUPS CHOPPED FRESH ITALIAN PARSLEY
1½ CUPS FRESH BASIL, SHREDDED
SALT AND PEPPER TO TASTE

SERVES 12

Cook the penne in rapidly boiling salted water for 10 minutes, or until done. When cooked, drain it well. Immediately toss the penne with the olive oil and allow them to cool.

Toss the pasta with the mozzarella, tomato, half the parsley and half the basil. Add salt and pepper to taste.

Garnish the pasta with the remaining chopped parsley and basil. Serve at room temperature.

EGGPLANT AGRO DOLCE

3 MEDIUM
  EGGPLANTS
1 CUP OLIVE OIL
½ CUP RED WINE
  VINEGAR
3 TABLESPOONS
  SUGAR
½ CUP CURRANTS
¼ CUP TOASTED
  PIGNOLI NUTS
½ CUP CHOPPED
  FRESH ITALIAN
  PARSLEY

SERVES 12

Wash and trim the eggplant. Cut it into a fine julienne.

Heat the olive oil in a large sauté pan over medium heat. Add the eggplant and cook for 6 minutes, or until the eggplant is soft.

Remove the eggplant from the heat and place it in a colander. Allow it to sit until all the excess oil has drained off. Place the eggplant in a serving bowl.

Combine the vinegar, sugar, and currants in a heavy saucepan over medium heat. Cook for about 10 minutes, stirring frequently, or until the liquid is syrupy. Add it to the drained eggplant and toss to combine. Sprinkle with pignoli nuts and parsley.

AMARETTO STUFFED PEARS

12 RIPE COMICE
  PEARS
¼ CUP FRESH LEMON
  JUICE
⅓ POUND ITALIAN
  AMARETTO
  COOKIES
1 TABLESPOON
  AMARETTO
  LIQUEUR
½ CUP UNSALTED
  BUTTER, MELTED
¼ CUP SUGAR
CREME ANGLAISE
  (SEE PAGE 207)
12 MINT SPRIGS

SERVES 12

Peel the pears, leaving the stems. Using a sharp knife or corer and working from the bottom of the pear, remove the core. Do not break through the stem end. Place the pears in cool water with the lemon juice as you work, to keep the pears from browning.

Preheat the oven to 375°. Generously butter a 9 x 12-inch baking dish (or any deep-sided dish large enough to hold 12 pears)

Crumble the cookies and stir in the Amaretto and 3 tablespoons of the melted butter until well combined. Drain one pear at a time and dry out the core. Stuff each with the Amaretto mixture and brush it with melted butter. Sprinkle it with sugar and place it in the prepared baking dish.

When all the pears are stuffed, add ½ cup water to the baking dish and bake, uncovered, for 45 minutes, or until the pears are tender and caramel-colored. *Do not overcook.*

Coat the bottom of a serving platter with Crème Anglaise and place the pears on top. Serve them warm or at room temperature, garnished with mint sprigs.

PEACHES UNDER BAROLO

Place the peeled peaches in a shallow bowl and sprinkle them with the sugar. Pour the Barolo wine over the peaches. Cover and refrigerate for 8 hours.

Serve the peaches in the wine marinade at room temperature.

12 LARGE RIPE
   PEACHES, PEELED
2 TABLESPOONS
   LIGHT BROWN
   SUGAR
4 CUPS BAROLO WINE

SERVES 12

Amaretto Stuffed Pears and Peaches under Barolo.

A Birthday Party for Mickey Mouse

MINIATURE CRAB EMPANADAS

VEGETABLE TACOS

TACO TARTLETS

GUACAMOLE

FRUIT WITH LEMON MAPLE DRESSING

PRALINES

PEANUT BUTTER COOKIES

DIVINITY

BROWNIES

POPCORN BALLS

CHOCOLATE FONDANT MICE

The chance to throw a birthday bash for Mickey Mouse was a wish come true. Since everyone loves a boat ride, a paddleboat was chosen—reminiscent of Mickey's early years on the river. But, he didn't have the magnificent skyline of Manhattan as his backdrop.

After a concert by the Disney Band, the guests, including many children, were invited into the boat's main dining salon. Fun food was the theme, and fantasy land was the decor. Color, not cost, was what made it all work.

Mickey and his friends danced away, with young and old alike. As the guests disembarked, we noticed the gleam in their eyes and realized that birthdays are truly for children of all ages.

Catching a child's eye invites the imagination to soar.

MINIATURE CRAB EMPANADAS

1 TABLESPOON UNSALTED BUTTER
2 TABLESPOONS MINCED ONION
1 TEASPOON MINCED FRESH GARLIC
2 TABLESPOONS MINCED FRESH PLUM TOMATO
⅓ POUND LUMP CRAB MEAT
2 TEASPOONS MINCED FRESH ITALIAN PARSLEY
½ TEASPOON CHOPPED CAPERS

Preheat the oven to 375°.

Heat the butter in a medium sauté pan over low heat. Add the onion, garlic, and tomato. Raise the heat to medium and sauté for 4 minutes, or until the vegetables are soft. Add the crab meat, parsley, capers, tomato paste, lemon juice, sugar, Tabasco sauce, and enough bread crumbs to hold the mixture together. Cook for 3 more minutes. Remove from the heat and allow to cool.

Roll the Tart Dough out ⅛-inch thick on a lightly floured board and cut it into 2½-inch circles. Place 1 teaspoon of filling in the center of each circle. Wet the edge of each circle with cold water and fold it in half. Seal by pressing the edges with the tines of a fork.

Whisk together the egg and cold water. Brush the tops of the empanadas and place them on a greased cookie sheet. Bake for 15 minutes, or until golden. Serve warm.

1 TEASPOON TOMATO PASTE
DASH FRESH LEMON JUICE
SUGAR TO TASTE
TABASCO SAUCE TO TASTE
2 TABLESPOONS PLAIN BREAD CRUMBS
TART DOUGH (SEE PAGE 29)
1 LARGE EGG
3 TABLESPOONS COLD WATER

SERVES 12

VEGETABLE TACOS

¾ POUND PLUM TOMATOES, SEEDED AND CHOPPED
½ CUP SEEDED AND DICED GREEN PEPPER
½ CUP SEEDED AND DICED RED PEPPER
¼ JALAPENO PEPPER, SEEDED, DEVEINED, AND MINCED
½ TEASPOON MINCED GARLIC

Mix together the tomato, peppers, garlic, onion, spices, Tabasco, salsa, and salt and pepper to taste. Let set for about 15 minutes. Then drain off excess liquid. Spoon the mixture into the Taco Shells and garnish with the grated cheese.

¼ CUP DICED ONION
SPRINKLE OF OREGANO
½ TEASPOON GROUND CUMIN
¼ TEASPOON TABASCO SAUCE
2 TABLESPOONS SALSA*
SALT AND PEPPER TO TASTE
12 TACO SHELLS
½ CUP GRATED SHARP CHEDDAR

SERVES 12

Tacos are a marvelous finger food for children.

TACO SHELLS

3 CUPS MASA HARINA (CORN MEAL FLOUR)*
1 TABLESPOON ALL-PURPOSE FLOUR
¼ TEASPOON BAKING POWDER
½ TEASPOON SALT
2 CUPS LUKEWARM WATER
1 CUP LARD
1 CUP CORN OIL

Combine the Masa Harina, flour, baking powder, salt, and water using a fork. When well combined, form the dough into a ball that is smooth to the touch. Cover and let it sit for 1 hour.

Divide the dough into 12 balls 1 inch in diameter. With your fingers, or using a small greased muffin tin as a mold, form the balls into 1-inch "bowls."

Heat the lard and oil together in a small, deep saucepan over high heat. When the oil reaches 365° on a cooking thermometer, deep-fry the taco shells for about 1 minute, or until golden. Remove them from the oil and drain on paper towels.

NOTE: INGREDIENTS MARKED WITH AN ASTERISK (*) CAN BE FOUND IN MEXICAN OR SPANISH GROCERIES.

TACO TARTLETS

¼ POUND UNSALTED TORTILLA CHIPS
¼ CUP PLUS 2 TABLESPOONS SOUR CREAM
2 TABLESPOONS TACO SAUCE
1 TABLESPOON CHOPPED BLACK OLIVES
½ POUND GROUND BEEF
1 TABLESPOON TACO-SEASONING MIX

2 TABLESPOONS MINCED SCALLIONS
1 TEASPOON ONION POWDER
1 TABLESPOON ICE WATER
½ CUP GRATED MILD CHEDDAR
⅛ CUP SLICED PICKLED JALAPENO PEPPERS

SERVES 12

Preheat the oven to 425°.

Coarsely chop the tortilla chips. Combine the chopped chips, ¼ cup of the sour cream, the taco sauce, and the olives until well blended. Set aside.

Mix together the ground beef, taco-seasoning mix, scallions, onion powder, and ice water. Line miniature muffin cups with a "shell" of the beef mixture.

Place 1 teaspoonful of the chip filling in each shell, mounding it slightly.

Bake the tartlets for 10 minutes, or until the shell is baked and the filling is firm. Sprinkle with the grated cheese and bake for an additional 2 minutes.

Remove from the oven and let it set for about 5 minutes. Remove taco tartlets from the pan. Garnish each with a dab of the remaining sour cream and a slice of pickled jalapeño pepper. Serve warm.

GUACAMOLE

3 VERY RIPE AVOCADOS
¾ CUP CHOPPED ONION
1 TEASPOON FRESH MINCED GARLIC
½ POUND PLUM TOMATOES, SEEDED AND DICED

1 TEASPOON FRESH LIME JUICE
SALT AND PEPPER TO TASTE
½ TEASPOON CHILI POWDER
¾ POUND TORTILLA CHIPS

SERVES 12

Peel, pit, and chop the avocados. Stir in the onion, garlic, tomato, and lime juice. Add salt and pepper and chili powder to taste. Place the avocado pit in the guacamole to prevent it from browning. Remove it before serving.

Let sit for 30 minutes, then taste and adjust the seasonings. Serve with tortilla chips.

FRUIT WITH LEMON MAPLE DRESSING

2 KIWIS
2 ORANGES
1 PINEAPPLE
1 HONEYDEW MELON
1 CANTALOUPE
2 RED DELICIOUS
  APPLES
1 PINT
  STRAWBERRIES
1 PINT BLUEBERRIES
LEMON MAPLE
  DRESSING

SERVES 12

Peel the kiwis and slice them across the grain into circles. Peel all the pith from the oranges and divide them into segments, discarding all the membrane.

Peel and core the pineapple and apples cut them into slices. Cut the honeydew and cantaloupe into balls.

Wash, dry, and stem the strawberries and slice them in half. Wash and dry the blueberries.

Arrange the fruit in an attractive pattern on a serving platter. Drizzle Lemon Maple Dressing over all and serve with additional dressing on the side.

LEMON MAPLE DRESSING

¾ CUP PURE MAPLE
  SYRUP
⅓ CUP FRESH LEMON
  JUICE

Combine the syrup, lemon juice, and paprika in a small bowl and whisk to blend. Gently fold in the whipped cream. Use immediately.

½ TEASPOON
  HUNGARIAN
  PAPRIKA
¾ CUP HEAVY CREAM,
  WHIPPED

Goofy shares the spotlight.

Make a wish.

PRALINES

2 CUPS GRANULATED
  SUGAR
1 CUP MAPLE SUGAR
¾ CUP WATER
¾ POUND CHOPPED
  PECANS
¾ POUND CHOPPED
  CASHEWS

SERVES 12

Preheat the oven to 350°.

Combine the sugars and water in a heavy saucepan over high heat. When the sugar has dissolved and the liquid is boiling, cover and cook for 3 minutes. Uncover and continue to boil, stirring frequently, until a candy thermometer registers 330°.

Place the saucepan in a shallow cold-water bath and quickly stir in the nuts. Pour the candy onto a greased baking sheet and smooth it to uniform thickness. Let it set at least 1 hour, then break it into pieces to serve.

PEANUT BUTTER COOKIES

¼ CUP UNSALTED
  BUTTER
¾ CUP CHUNKY
  PEANUT BUTTER
½ CUP DARK BROWN
  SUGAR, TIGHTLY
  PACKED
1 CUP GRANULATED
  SUGAR
1 TEASPOON
  VANILLA EXTRACT
2 LARGE EGGS
2¼ CUPS ALL-
  PURPOSE FLOUR
½ TEASPOON BAKING
  SODA

MAKES 4 DOZEN

Using an electric mixer, cream the butter, peanut butter, sugars, and vanilla until light and fluffy. Beat in the eggs. Sift the flour and baking soda and gradually mix them into the batter. When blended, divide the dough into thirds and wrap it tightly in plastic. Freeze for 15 minutes, and then refrigerate for 30 minutes.

Preheat the oven to 400°.

Working quickly with cool hands, make 1-inch balls of dough. Place the balls on a greased cookie sheet about 2 inches apart and press them flat, in a grid pattern, with fork tines first dipped in flour.

Bake the cookies for 10 minutes, or until they are slightly browned around the edges. Remove them from the cookie sheet and cool them on a wire rack.

DIVINITY

Bring the sugar, syrup, water, and vinegar to a boil over high heat in a heavy saucepan. Cover and continue boiling for 3 minutes. Uncover and continue to boil, stirring frequently, until a candy thermometer reads 260°.

In the top half of a double boiler over hot water, whisk the egg whites. When the egg whites are firm, whisk in the hot sugar syrup.

Stir in the vanilla and fold in the nuts. Continue stirring over hot water until the candy begins to hold its shape. Remove it from the heat and form it into small, bite-sized balls. Cool them on waxed paper.

1 ⅓ CUPS SUGAR
⅓ CUP LIGHT CORN SYRUP
⅓ CUP WATER
1 ½ TEASPOONS WHITE VINEGAR
1 LARGE EGG WHITE
⅛ TEASPOON VANILLA EXTRACT
1 CUP CHOPPED PISTACHIOS

SERVES 12

The dining salon awaits Mickey's friends.

Mouse heaven—Chocolate Fondant Mice atop a mountain of Brownies with marzipan cheese.

BROWNIES

1 CUP ALL-PURPOSE
  FLOUR
1¾ CUPS SUGAR
½ TEASPOON BAKING
  POWDER
1 CUP COCOA
  POWDER
½ CUP UNSALTED
  BUTTER
4 LARGE EGGS

Preheat the oven to 350°.

Butter and flour a 9 x 13-inch baking pan. Set it aside.

In a food processor, using the metal blade, combine the flour, sugar, baking powder, and cocoa powder. When well blended, cut in the butter to make a coarse meal.

Beat the eggs with the vanilla and quickly stir them into the flour mixture. Remove the batter from the processor and stir in the chocolate pieces and nuts.

Pour the batter into the prepared pan and bake for 25 minutes, or until the edges pull away from the pan. Cool the pan on a wire rack. Cut the brownies into squares to serve.

2½ TEASPOONS
  VANILLA EXTRACT
¾ CUP SEMISWEET
  CHOCOLATE
  PIECES
½ CUP CHOPPED
  PECANS
½ CUP CHOPPED
  WALNUTS

SERVES 12

POPCORN BALLS

Place the popcorn in a large bowl greased with the butter. Set it in a warm spot.

Bring the syrup, vinegar, and salt to a boil in a heavy saucepan over high heat, stirring frequently, until the syrup reaches 250° on a candy thermometer. Stir in the vanilla and remove the mixture from the heat.

Pour the syrup over the popcorn, mixing with a greased fork until the popcorn is thoroughly coated. Working quickly, wet your hands and form the popcorn into 12 2½-inch balls.

When cool, wrap the balls in clear plastic wrap. Store them at room temperature.

3 QUARTS UNSALTED, POPPED POPCORN
2 TABLESPOONS UNSALTED BUTTER
2 CUPS "LITE" CORN SYRUP
1 TABLESPOON WHITE VINEGAR
½ TEASPOON SALT
1 TABLESPOON VANILLA EXTRACT

SERVES 12

CHOCOLATE FONDANT MICE

Bring the sugar, glucose, and water to a boil in a medium saucepan over high heat. Stir until the sugar dissolves. Cover and boil for 3 more minutes. Then uncover and continue to boil, stirring frequently, until a candy thermometer registers 240°. Immediately place the pan in ice water and stir for 1 minute.

Spread the fondant out on a cold surface (preferably a marble pastry board) and let it set for 3 minutes. Then begin to work it back and forth and into itself with a spatula. Continue working the fondant for 10 minutes, or until it becomes crumbly. When crumbling begins, dampen your hands and knead the fondant until it is moist and smooth.

Form the fondant into a ball and place it in a non-reactive bowl that has been sprinkled with cold water. Cover it with a damp towel and set in a cool place for 12 hours.

Melt the chocolate in the top half of a double boiler over boiling water. Add the vanilla and remove it from the heat. Allow to cool slightly, then knead the mixture into the fondant. When well combined, form the fondant into 1¼-inch balls. Using your fingers, mold each ball into an oval mouse shape and form ears. Stick a piece of silk cord into the round end for the tail and silver dragées into the head for eyes. Let the mice harden for 1 hour before serving.

1 CUP SUGAR
1 TEASPOON GLUCOSE
⅓ CUP COLD WATER
6 OUNCES SEMISWEET CHOCOLATE
½ TEASPOON VANILLA EXTRACT
AT LEAST 12 4-INCH LENGTHS FINE SILK CORD
AT LEAST 24 SILVER DRAGEES

SERVES 12

A Japanese Picnic at the Botanic Garden

NAPA ROLLS

ASPARAMAKI

YELLOWTAIL AND PINK SNAPPER SASHIMI

TEKKAMAKI

OSHINKO

SMOKED DUCK AND BUCKWHEAT NOODLES

JAPANESE TOMATO SALAD

ASSORTED JAPANESE SWEETS

The color, texture, and arrangement of Japanese dishes are often inspired by the simple, beautiful containers in which they are served. When a *bento*, or Japanese picnic box, is planned, the container as well as the contents must create a visual feast, in harmony with other food being presented. Seen in relation to its surroundings, the *bento* must not compete with nature.

The first blush of spring is an auspicious time for a picnic. This party, held in the Japanese section of the Brooklyn Botanic Gardens, has nature as its decor. The subtle flavors of sushi and sashimi refresh the palate between bites of pungent oshinko, and sips of sake. The meal is rounded out with sweets as delicate as cherry blossoms.

Local Japanese restaurants and suppliers were asked to provide the sashimi, oshinko, and sweets.

Nature provides the serene setting in a Japanese garden.

NAPA ROLLS

2 LARGE EGG YOLKS

2 TEASPOONS WASABI POWDER*

¼ TEASPOON SALT

1 CUP VEGETABLE OIL

¼ CUP RICE WINE VINEGAR*

2 TABLESPOONS FRESH LIME JUICE

20 LARGE NAPA CABBAGE LEAVES*

¼ POUND LARGE CALIFORNIA SPINACH LEAVES

½ POUND CARROTS

½ POUND SHIITAKE MUSHROOMS*

¼ CUP SOY SAUCE

1½ TEASPOONS SUGAR

¾ CUP WATER

½ TEASPOON DASHI*

3 TABLESPOONS SESAME SEEDS

SERVES 12

In a food processor, using the metal blade, combine the egg yolks, wasabi powder, and salt. With the motor running, slowly pour in the vegetable oil in a steady stream to make a thick mayonnaise. Quickly stir in 1 tablespoon of the rice wine vinegar and the lime juice. Remove the mixture from the processor bowl and set it aside.

Trim the cabbage leaves and cut away any thick parts. Trim the stems from the spinach leaves. Place the cabbage and spinach in a pot of rapidly boiling salted water for 30 seconds, or until just wilted. Immediately remove them to iced water. When they are cool, drain and pat them dry. Lay them out on paper towels so that all the extra moisture is absorbed.

Peel and cut the carrots into a thick julienne. Place them in rapidly boiling salted water for 1 minute, or until just cooked but still crisp. Immediately remove them to iced water. When they are cool, drain and pat them dry.

Remove the stems from the mushrooms and reserve them for another use. Slice the mushroom caps into a thick julienne.

Bring the soy sauce, sugar, water, dashi, and remaining rice wine vinegar to a boil in a small saucepan over high heat. Add the mushrooms and remove the pan from the heat. Cover it and let it set for 10 minutes. Drain the mushroom julienne and pat it dry.

Using a sushi mat as a base, spread out the cabbage leaves in one layer to make a rectangle about 8 x 5 inches.

Top the cabbage with spinach leaves to cover. Lightly coat the spinach leaves with the wasabi mayonnaise.

Lay the carrot julienne in a single line about ½ inch from the long edge. Lay a line of the mushroom julienne next to the carrot line.

Roll the leaves up tightly, making an 8-inch-long roll. Secure it with rubber bands or encase it in clear plastic wrap. Refrigerate for at least 1 hour.

When ready to serve, remove the rubber bands or plastic wrap and slice the roll into 1-inch pieces, cutting them slightly on the diagonal. Sprinkle each piece with sesame seeds and serve immediately.

NOTE: INGREDIENTS MARKED WITH AN ASTERISK (*) CAN BE FOUND IN ORIENTAL SPECIALTY STORES AND MARKETS.

Bento *box.*

ASPARAMAKI

4 VERY THIN SLICES
 BEEF TENDERLOIN,
 EACH 4 X 1½
 INCHES
4 4-INCH-LONG
 ASPARAGUS
 HEADS, WELL
 TRIMMED
½ TEASPOON
 VEGETABLE OIL

Wrap the beef slices around the asparagus to cover. Secure them with a toothpick inserted diagonally.

Heat the oil in a sauté pan over medium heat. Add the beef rolls, seam side down, and cook, turning often, for about 2 minutes, or until the beef has begun to change color. Immediately add the remaining ingredients and cook for 2 more minutes.

Remove the rolls and slice, crosswise, into thirds. Serve immediately or cool and serve at room temperature.

½ TABLESPOON SAKE
1¼ TABLESPOONS
 SOY SAUCE
½ TABLESPOON
 SUGAR
½ TABLESPOON COLD
 WATER

MAKES 12

TEKKAMAKI

Wash the rice and place it in a heavy saucepan with a lid. Add the boiling water and cover tightly. Bring the rice to a boil over medium heat. Reduce the heat to low and cook for 15 minutes, or until all the liquid is absorbed.

Turn off the flame but keep the saucepan tightly covered on the burner, with the lid wrapped in a kitchen towel, for an additional 15 minutes.

Dissolve the sugar and salt in the vinegar in a small saucepan over low heat. When the sugar and salt are dissolved, remove the pan from the heat and allow it to cool to room temperature.

Using a flat wooden spoon or spatula, spread the hot rice in a thin layer across the bottom of a wooden bowl. Toss the rice with horizontal, cutting strokes, without mashing the grains. Gradually sprinkle the dressing over the rice (but do not let the rice get soggy), fanning the rice to cool it quickly as you sprinkle.

Cut the tuna into ¼-inch strips.

With wet fingers, spread the rice onto the Nori. Smear it with a faint line of wasabi paste and place a strip of tuna on top. Roll the Nori tightly and slice it into 1-inch serving pieces. Keep the pieces refrigerated until ready to use.

¾ CUP SUSHI RICE*
1 CUP BOILING
 WATER
4 TEASPOONS SUGAR
DASH SALT
1 TABLESPOON RICE
 WINE VINEGAR*
½ POUND TUNA
2 SHEETS NORI
 (SEAWEED FOR
 SUSHI)*
4 OUNCES WASABI
 PASTE*

SERVES 12

Smoked Duck and Buckwheat Noodles.

Oshinko—pickled vegetables.

SMOKED DUCK
AND BUCKWHEAT NOODLES

1 TEASPOON DASHI*
¼ CUP WATER
½ CUP SOY SAUCE
⅓ CUP RICE WINE
    VINEGAR*
½ CUP SUGAR
1 ¼ TEASPOONS
    SESAME OIL
3 LARGE EGGS
1 TABLESPOONS
    CORN OIL
¾ POUND
    BUCKWHEAT
    NOODLES
½ POUND SHIITAKE
    MUSHROOMS,
    JULIENNED*
2 CUPS JULIENNED
    CUCUMBER
3 CUPS JULIENNED
    SMOKED DUCK*
¼ CUP CHOPPED
    SCALLIONS

SERVES 12

Combine the dashi and water in a small saucepan over medium heat. Bring to a simmer and cook for 3 minutes. Lower the heat.

Add the soy sauce, vinegar, ¼ cup sugar, and sesame oil. Bring to a simmer and cook for 5 minutes. Remove from the heat and allow to cool. Refrigerate the dressing until ready to use.

Beat the eggs with the remaining sugar.

Heat the oil in a heavy saucepan over medium heat and immediately pour in the eggs. Let them cook in the form of a pancake until brown around the edges. Flip, and brown the other side. Remove the pancake from the heat and cut it into a julienne.

Pour the noodles into rapidly boiling salted water and cook them for 7 minutes, or until cooked. Drain and toss the noodles into cold water. Drain them again.

When the noodles are well drained, toss in half of the dashi dressing and place them on a serving platter. Arrange the julienned pancake, mushrooms, cucumbers, and smoked duck around the sides and sprinkle the chopped scallions over all. Drizzle with the remaining dressing. Serve immediately.

Japanese Tomato Salad.

Sashimi.

JAPANESE TOMATO SALAD

14 MEDIUM SHIITAKE
   MUSHROOMS*
5 TABLESPOONS
   SESAME OIL
¼ CUP LIGHT SOY
   SAUCE
¼ CUP RICE VINEGAR*
8 LARGE, FIRM, RIPE
   TOMATOES

Cut the mushrooms into juliennes. Heat 1 tablespoon of the sesame oil in a medium sauté pan over low heat. Add the mushrooms and sauté for 1 minute. Remove them to a bowl and add the soy sauce, vinegar, and remaining oil. Allow to cool.

Peel, core, and seed the tomatoes. Cut them into ½-inch cubes and set aside.

Wash and trim off the green part of the scallions. Thinly slice the white part crosswise. Set aside.

When the mushrooms are cool, toss in the scallions and ginger. Add the tomatoes and daikon and gently toss to combine. Cover and refrigerate the salad for at least 30 minutes before serving.

6 SCALLIONS
1½ TABLESPOONS
   GRATED GINGER
   ROOT
2 CUPS JULIENNED
   DAIKON (JAPANESE
   WHITE RADISH)*

SERVES 12

SIGHT
and
SOUND

AT A SUCCESSFUL PARTY, THE GUESTS ARE HAPPILY UNAWARE OF ANY TROUBLE THE HOST HAS taken to set the stage: Lovely surroundings and wonderful music, well suited to the theme, appear perfectly natural, directing attention to conversation, dancing, eating, and creating warm memories. The best hosts know that such an effect can only be achieved by carefully planning the decor, lighting, and music. From private party to large public gathering, these mood-enhancers subtly give an event its unique character.

For private celebrations, surround yourself with things that you love. Instead of changing the look of your home, enhance it. If you don't have a room large enough to entertain in, try using a tent on your lawn. Convert it into that faraway place of your dreams.

In deciding what to highlight indoors, think of each room as a photograph in a magazine. Note what objects or flowers or small arrangements would catch your interest. Highlight these, and this is often all you will need to set the stage for entertaining. Flowers and plants will make your home come alive, welcoming your guests and adding impact through color and freshness. Arrange them to reflect your style, whether it be in full, lush, bouquets modeled after Dutch paintings, or in the spare, elegant sprays of Japanese *ikebana*.

You can use tabletop decorations to set the theme, as long as they don't interfere with dining and good conversation. This is one way in which you can transform your setting

Through the use of lighting and candles, the lobby of an office building
magically converts into a gala party space.

Music is the inspiration for every Carnegie Hall gala.

without changing the decor of your home. Once your guests are seated at tables, their focus narrows. The circle of guests at the table becomes a self-contained universe. Transport the diners to Victorian England, the American Southwest, or ancient Etruria through the tabletop design of your choice.

Prepare the tabletop to complement the look of the food you will serve as well as the party's theme. In selecting linens, concentrate on their color, texture, and sheen. When planning centerpieces, pay attention to their height, density, and quality. Highlight the center of the table. Try a variety of small containers rather than one large bouquet. Consider using objects or memorabilia rather than flowers. Place keepsakes in new and novel combinations. Vegetables can make a dramatic centerpiece; look for contrasting shapes, colors, and textures in arranging them. Experiment with interesting napkin folds. When entertaining at home, the only restric-

tions should be that of your own good taste.

For parties outside of your own home, you will probably need to reshape the environment to suit your theme and reflect your goals. Corporate entertaining often involves a promotional display of products or services. The mood you set for a political fund-raiser will be substantially different from that for a society benefit: For a political event, the candidate or cause will have a dominant presence but for a society benefit, the emphasis should shift onto the guests.

Business and benefit dinners have a few guidelines. Set the corporate tables in a crisp and straightforward style, without any distractions. Choose china, linens, and flatware in classic designs and colors, more tonal than bright. Dress the tables with flowers, also keeping the design classic. For social events, design more extravagant forms of table decor that reflect the gala quality of the evening. Remember that tabletops create a focus for the many small parties going on within the framework of the larger event.

Welcome tables should be draped in warm, friendly colors, graced with flowers, and displaying subtle corporate or benefit identification. Staff them with friendly greeters to assist the guests. Arrange place cards attractively and accessibly.

For any dinner party, it helps to familiarize yourself with some basic rules of table-setting etiquette:

1. Always pad the tables when using a linen cloth to protect the china and glassware as well as to cut down on dining room noise.

2. Place the napkins in the center of the place setting or on a service plate. If there will be a preset appetizer course, place the napkins on the left side of the plate.

3. Position the place cards either above the service plate, in the center of the place setting, or on top of the formal napkin. For informal dinners, you can use first names only on the place cards. For formal dinners, use full names. Always be sure the names are written clearly.

4. Never set more than three courses of flatware on a table. Reset as needed.

5. A show plate is not necessary at an informal dinner.

More than any other element in your environment, lighting creates and sustains the mood. It can soften through shadow or electrify with brightness, open up spaces, and add warmth and friendliness. Whether the glow is cast from a warm, blazing fireplace or from spotlights on a beautiful table, lighting makes an environmental statement.

Candles are perhaps the most magical way to set the mood. Votive candles create a beautiful effect, reflecting in the water and wine glasses, and shimmering against the silverware. They last a long time and rarely blow out. The reflected glow from votive candles is also most flattering to diners. In the spring tapered candle shades can be covered with leaves and flowers or, for the winter, the tapers can be encased in hurricane shades. Shaded tapers produce extraordinary down-lighting on flowers and center-

The decor sets the theme and creates the environment.

185

Performance as the center of an event.

Art, flowers, and music.

pieces. Short, thick candles floating in bowls of water surrounded by flowers create wonderfully reflective centerpieces. Whatever the style, always choose unscented candles to avoid competing with the aromas of food. Light the candles before the guests enter the dining room. (Never use candles at midday.)

At cocktail parties, keep the lights bright and white, because people tend to be more talkative in brightly lit spaces. Use softer lighting when you want to move guests into the dining area from the cocktail setting.

Lighting is perhaps the most effective way to create a particular decor within large public spaces. Use pin-spot lighting to focus attention on architectural details or specific areas of the room. Patterns can also be projected on the walls to change textures. Casting the light upwards creates a dramatic theatrical effect and makes the ceiling seem higher. Down-lighting bathes a room in a warm glow. Use side-lighting to soften hard columns and produce shadowy effects. Make fountains and pools the central design elements by bathing them in the light of clear or colored votive candles.

If lighting helps set the mood through warmth, sound completes the scene—both the sound of music and the sound of laughter. In your home, plan the use of music carefully. Not every party is enhanced by music. Knowing when not to use it is

as important as using music effectively. Live music intensifies the experience, but before planning a musical interlude, make sure your rooms are large enough to accommodate musicians and guests comfortably. If the music is for dancing, is there space for dancing and talk? A less obtrusive option is a single instrument—a cello, a flute, or piano.

Taped music is another alternative, offering a wider range. If you're planning to dance, select a good assortment of different moods so that the music will help structure the evening.

Before you hire a disc jockey or musicians, if possible, you will want to observe how they perform and whether their style and music is right for you. Get written assurance from their booking agent that the musicians you heard will be the same ones who perform at your event. When planning a charity theme party in which the music relates to the theme, be certain that the booking agent is aware of your commitment to authenticity. The musicians must be able to play the selections you wish to hear. If you want an evening of waltzes, hire classical musicians. Great dance music makes the evening.

All musicians are rightfully proud of their work and seek an appreciative audience, but if you are using musicians in the background, make sure they understand that they are not the main event. When choosing dance music (for a wedding, for example),

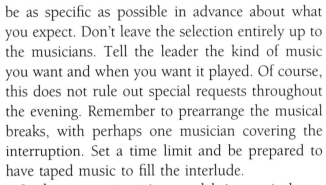

The warm glow of a tent at night.

An enraptured audience.

be as specific as possible in advance about what you expect. Don't leave the selection entirely up to the musicians. Tell the leader the kind of music you want and when you want it played. Of course, this does not rule out special requests throughout the evening. Remember to prearrange the musical breaks, with perhaps one musician covering the interruption. Set a time limit and be prepared to have taped music to fill the interlude.

In the corporate setting, a celebrity musical performer can be a special draw and add an extra dimension to your reception. If your guests are all of a similar age, book a musician they will remember from a particular era.

Music can enhance the theme of a corporate event. On the Fourth of July, banjos and barbershop quartets arouse feelings of patriotism and American spirit. What better introduction for a new computer program than the strains of electronic, new-age music? A string or woodwind quartet can provide a most pleasing background for a corporate dinner, with selections ranging from classical to contemporary. Harp and flute combinations are light, adding sparkle to lunch or brunch. The piano is a wonderful choice for a corporate cocktail reception.

Lively music is the foundation of the dinner dance or charity ball. At any ball, it is important that the music be continuous. As the evening progresses, the tempo should change. This gives guests a chance to try their fancy footwork, but also allows some guests to sit and talk. The music must never overpower the conversation or the dancing. Your guests, not the musicians, are the stars.

At every event, the most appreciated sound for a host is the spirited buzz of a room full of guests talking. Scintillating conversation will breathe life into your party. The great host creates an atmosphere in which conversations can flow. Toasts are another aspect of conversation and are often included to give guests an opportunity to share the spotlight. The toasts can be short and formal, or they can be spontaneous and full of emotion. Joy should never be suppressed. Conversation is the one memory of a party that each of us holds dear.

The time devoted to decor, lighting, and sound will greatly enhance your party. A pleasing, warmly lit environment, coupled with appropriate music and lively conversation set the stage for an enjoyable and memorable event.

Unusual Combinations

CORN AND CHIVE MADELEINES

CAROLINA SPICY SHRIMP

TOASTED RAVIOLI WITH TOMATO ROSEMARY
SAUCE

WOODLAND DUCK SALAD

SALMON AND SOLE CHECKERBOARD

FROZEN RASPBERRY SOUFFLE

This unusual menu with its ravishing hues reflects the host's creative eye. A graphic designer, Joe Lombardo celebrates a great love of color and texture in every aspect of his life. The atmosphere of creative disorder which he designed in the apartment invites guests to participate in his unique vision. Our host firmly believes that art asserts and expands the self.

His inspirational approach is evident in the inventive menu, with its bold selections—flavorful and distinctive. The textures are playful and the colors harmonious. Like all works of art, the meal, the tabletop, and the environment offered a·new perspective on the everyday world.

Style is highly connected to the visual sense.

CORN AND CHIVE MADELEINES

¼ CUP YELLOW CORNMEAL

⅓ CUP ALL-PURPOSE FLOUR

1 TEASPOON SUGAR

1 TEASPOON BAKING POWDER

PINCH CAYENNE PEPPER

1 TABLESPOON COLD VEGETABLE SHORTENING

Preheat the oven to 400°.

Combine the corn meal, flour, sugar, baking powder, and cayenne pepper. Blend in the cold shortening, using a pastry blender, to make a coarse meal. Quickly whisk in the egg and milk to make a loose batter. When well blended, stir in the dried chives.

Using melted butter, generously coat a mini-madeleine pan and fill each cup three quarters full. Place in the oven and bake for approximately 7 minutes or until golden brown.

Remove the madeleines from the pan and cool them on wire racks. When cool, top each madeleine with a dollop of crème fraîche and a dollop of golden caviar.

1 LARGE EGG

¼ CUP MILK

1 TABLESPOON DRIED CHIVES

¼ CUP CREME FRAICHE (AVAILABLE READY-MADE)

½ OUNCE GOLDEN CAVIAR

SERVES 12

CAROLINA SPICY SHRIMP

3 CUPS FRESH FISH STOCK (SEE PAGE 26)

½ CUP CORN OIL

¼ CUP CATSUP

¼ CUP CIDER VINEGAR

½ TABLESPOON WORCESTERSHIRE SAUCE

1½ TEASPOONS LIGHT BROWN SUGAR

Bring the Fish Stock to a boil.

In a bowl, combine the corn oil, catsup, vinegar, Worcestershire Sauce, sugar, salt, mustard, Tabasco sauce, and bay leaves. Set this marinade aside.

Place the shrimp in the rapidly boiling Fish Stock and cook for 3 minutes, or until the shrimp are bright pink and cooked. Drain.

Immediately toss the shrimp in the marinade. Add the onions. Cover and refrigerate them for at least 4 hours. Remove from the refrigerator just before serving.

¼ TEASPOON SALT

¼ TEASPOON DRY MUSTARD

¼ TEASPOON TABASCO SAUCE (OR TO TASTE)

3 BAY LEAVES

1½ POUNDS SHRIMP, PEELED AND DEVEINED

1 CUP ONION SLICES

SERVES 12

TOASTED RAVIOLI WITH TOMATO ROSEMARY SAUCE

1 CUP PLAIN BREADCRUMBS

½ CUP PARMESAN CHEESE

24 RICOTTA RAVIOLI (SEE PAGE 223)

Combine the breadcrumb and Parmesan cheese.

Dip each ravioli in milk, then toss in the breadcrumb and cheese mixture to cover completely.

Heat the oil to 365° in a deep fryer. Drop the ravioli into the oil, a few at a time, and fry for 2 minutes or until golden.

Drain them on paper towels. Serve hot with Tomato Rosemary Sauce.

⅔ CUP EVAPORATED MILK

4 CUPS CORN OIL

TOMATO ROSEMARY SAUCE

SERVES 12

TOMATO ROSEMARY SAUCE

1 TABLESPOON
   OLIVE OIL
½ POUND PLUM
   TOMATOES
1 TEASPOON MINCED
   GARLIC
PINCH RED PEPPER
   FLAKES
1 TABLESPOON
   TOMATO PASTE

Heat the olive oil in a medium sauté pan over low heat. Add the tomato, garlic, and red pepper flakes. Raise the heat and sauté for 10 minutes. Add the tomato paste, rosemary, sugar, and salt and pepper. Simmer for 10 more minutes. Remove from the heat and fold in the parsley.

Serve at room temperature.

¼ TEASPOON DRIED
   ROSEMARY
PINCH SUGAR
SALT AND PEPPER
   TO TASTE
2 TABLESPOONS
   CHOPPED FRESH
   ITALIAN PARSLEY

A table set with elegance and whimsey.

WOODLAND DUCK SALAD

3 WHOLE DUCK
  BREASTS

SALT AND PEPPER
  TO TASTE

⅛ POUND DRIED
  PORCINI
  MUSHROOMS

¼ POUND SHIITAKE
  MUSHROOMS

¼ POUND
  CHANTERELLE
  MUSHROOMS

½ CUP WALNUT OIL

3 TABLESPOONS
  UNSALTED
  BUTTER

2 CUPS ¼-INCH
  SQUARE FRENCH
  BREAD CROUTONS

¼ POUND CANADIAN
  BACON, CUT INTO
  ⅛-INCH CUBES

3 LARGE ORANGES

2 BUNCHES
  RADICCHIO

2 BUNCHES FRISEE
  (OR CHICORY)

2 HEADS BOSTON
  LETTUCE

¼ CUP MINCED
  FRESH SHALLOTS

¾ CUP RASPBERRY
  VINEGAR

1 PINT FRESH
  RASPBERRIES

SERVES 12

Preheat the oven to 400°.

Remove the skin from each duck breast. Place the skin in a shallow roasting pan and bake for 15 minutes. Remove from the oven and pour off all but 1 tablespoon of the fat. Discard the skin. Cut the breasts in halves, brush them with the melted fat, and season with salt and pepper. Place in a roasting pan and roast them for about 3 minutes per side, or until the outside is brown but the center is still rare. Remove from the oven and cool on wire racks. When cool, slice the breasts on the bias and set aside.

Place the porcini mushrooms in 2 cups of boiling water and let set for about 5 minutes, or until reconstituted. Drain well and slice.

Keeping them separated, slice the shiitake and chanterelle mushrooms. Heat 1 tablespoon of the walnut oil and 1 tablespoon of the butter in a medium sauté pan over low heat. Sauté the mushrooms, one type at a time, for 6 minutes, or until they have wilted and their juices have started to evaporate. Remove from the pan with a slotted spoon and set aside, still keeping each kind of mushroom separate.

Add the croutons to the sauté pan (with more butter if necessary), and gently sauté them for 3 minutes, or until golden. Set the croutons aside.

Add the bacon cubes to the sauté pan and cook for 5 minutes, or until crisp. Drain and set them aside.

Peel and section the oranges, being certain that all the white pith, membrane, and seeds are removed. Set them aside.

Wash the lettuces and tear the leaves into bite-sized pieces. Drain and dry thoroughly. Set aside.

In a small sauté pan, over medium heat, melt the remaining butter. Add the shallots and cook them for 2 minutes, or until the shallots have wilted. Remove them from the pan and place in the bowl of a food processor.

In the food processor, with a metal blade, combine the raspberry vinegar, remaining walnut oil, salt and pepper with the shallots. Process until well combined.

Arrange equal portions of the lettuces on each of the 12 serving plates. Sprinkle with the bacon and croutons. Place a small mound of each kind of mushroom on the edge of each plate. Form a pinwheel of duck slices in the center and garnish with raspberries and orange sections. Drizzle vinaigrette over all.

Salmon and Sole Checkerboard

Preheat the oven to 350°.

Cut the sole and salmon fillets into ½ x 4-inch strips. Using 3 strips of sole and 3 strips of salmon, weave the strips together to form a red-and-white square. Make 12 squares of fish.

Butter a baking sheet with sides. Carefully place the fish squares on it, leaving about 2 inches between each. Pour on enough of the Fish Stock to come up about ¼ inch in the pan. Cover with lightly buttered waxed paper. Place in the oven and bake for about 12 minutes, or until the fish squares are well set and cooked through.

While the fish squares are baking, heat half of the remaining butter in a sauté pan over low heat. Add the diced tomato and gently warm. Add salt and pepper. Remove the pan from the heat and keep it warm.

Sauté the julienned zucchini in the same manner using the remaining butter. Keep warm.

When the fish is done, remove it from the oven and let it set for about 1 minute.

Coat the surface of each serving plate with a generous portion of the Ginger Sauce. Place a fish square on the center of each plate, the warm diced tomatoes at the left top corner, and the julienned zucchini at the bottom right corner. Brush the fish squares with clarified butter and serve them immediately.

3 POUNDS FRESH LEMON SOLE FILLET

5½ POUNDS FRESH SALMON FILLET

½ CUP UNSALTED BUTTER

3 CUPS FRESH FISH STOCK (SEE PAGE 26)

4 LARGE TOMATOES, PEELED, SEEDED, AND FINELY DICED

SALT AND PEPPER TO TASTE

3 LARGE ZUCCHINI, JULIENNED

GINGER SAUCE

¼ CUP CLARIFIED BUTTER

SERVES 12

GINGER SAUCE

5 CUPS FRESH FISH STOCK (SEE PAGE 126)

1¼ CUPS DRY WHITE WINE

2½ TABLESPOONS MINCED FRESH GINGER ROOT

Place the Fish Stock, wine, ginger root, and shallots in a non-reactive saucepan over medium heat. Bring them to a boil. Lower the heat and continue cooking the sauce until it has reduced by two-thirds. Remove from the heat and strain.

Return the sauce to the heat and stir in the cream and cognac. Cook over medium heat, stirring frequently, for 10 minutes—until it has reduced enough to coat a spoon. Remove the sauce from the heat and keep it warm until ready to serve.

2 TABLESPOONS MINCED FRESH SHALLOTS

4 CUPS HEAVY CREAM

¼ CUP COGNAC

A combination for the eye as well as the palate.

Frozen Raspberry Souffle

20 OUNCES FROZEN
    RASPBERRIES
¼ CUP FRESH LEMON
    JUICE
2 CUPS SUGAR
1 CUP COLD WATER
10 LARGE EGG
    WHITES
⅛ TEASPOON CREAM
    OF TARTAR
2 CUPS HEAVY
    CREAM
NUTTED MERINGUES
⅔ CUP SLICED
    ALMONDS

SERVES 12

Cut a piece of waxed paper 10-inches wide and 3-inches longer than the circumference of a 9 x 2¾-inch spring-form pan. Fold the paper in half lengthwise and grease both sides with butter or vegetable oil. Line the inside of the pan with the oiled paper, leaving a 2-inch collar above the rim.

Drain the raspberries and purée them in a food processor, using the metal blade, for 10 to 15 seconds. Add the lemon juice and pulse 3 times to combine. Set aside.

Bring the sugar and water to a boil in a heavy saucepan over medium heat. Boil without stirring until the syrup reaches 260° on a candy thermometer.

Beat the egg whites until foamy in a large mixing bowl at low speed. Add the cream of tartar and beat at a high speed until stiff peaks are formed. Continue beating, adding the sugar syrup in a steady stream. Beat until the meringue is cool, about 25 minutes. Transfer the meringue to an 8-quart mixing bowl and gently fold in the raspberry purée.

Whip the cream until stiff and gently fold it into the raspberry mixture.

Place 1 baked Nutted Meringue in the bottom of the prepared spring-form pan, trimming it to fit. Spoon in enough of the raspberry mixture to form a 2-inch layer. Smooth the top with a spatula and cover with a second baked Nutted Meringue. Tap the pan gently on the counter to eliminate any air bubbles. Spoon in the remaining raspberry mixture and smooth the top. Freeze, uncovered, for at least 4 hours, but preferably overnight.

Just before serving the soufflé, remove the side of the spring-form pan and the waxed paper collar. Place the soufflé on a serving platter. Gently press the sliced almonds on the top.

To serve, cut the soufflé into thin slices.

NUTTED MERINGUES

¼ CUP BLANCHED
    ALMONDS
¼ CUP HAZELNUTS,
    SHELLED
½ CUP PLUS 2
    TABLESPOONS
    SUPER FINE
    SUGAR
2½ TEASPOONS
    CORNSTARCH

Preheat the oven to 350°.

Cut two 9-inch parchment paper (baking paper) circles and, with a pencil, trace an 8¾-inch circle on each. Invert the parchment circles onto 2 separate baking sheets. Set them aside.

Place the nuts in separate pans and bake for 8 to 10 minutes, or until lightly browned. Cool completely. Rub the hazelnuts with a kitchen towel to remove as much of the skin as possible. Reduce the oven to 275°.

In a food processor, using the metal blade, blend the nuts, ½ cup of the sugar, and the cornstarch for about 1 minute, or until the nuts are finely chopped.

3 LARGE EGG WHITES
⅛ TEASPOON CREAM
    OF TARTAR
½ TEASPOON
    VANILLA EXTRACT
⅛ TEASPOON
    ALMOND EXTRACT
PINCH OF SALT

MAKES 2

Beat the egg whites until foamy. Add the remaining sugar, extracts, cream of tartar, and salt, and continue beating until firm peaks form. Fold into the nut mixture.

Fit a pastry bag with a ½-inch tip and fill it with the meringue. To keep the paper circles from sliding, secure them to the baking sheet with a dab of the meringue. Pipe a circle on each piece of parchment paper following the 8¾-inch penciled lines. Fill in with the remaining meringue in concentric circles, starting in the center of the circle.

Bake the meringues for 1 hour and 15 minutes or until they are dry and firm to the touch. Remove them from the oven and invert them onto wire cooling racks. When completely cool, remove the parchment paper.

When guests are greeted in this foyer, they know that they are in store for fun.

A Loft Wedding

DILLED SCALLOP TERRINE WITH CUCUMBER
LEEK SAUCE

BREAST OF DUCK WITH CHARTREUSE

ZUCCHINI AND POTATOES ANNA

SAUTEED WATERCRESS AND RED RADISHES

SPECIALTY WEDDING CAKE

CHOCOLATE DIPPED STRAWBERRIES

The clean, white space of a loft with its airy feeling and fresh modern look especially appealed to the bride and groom, both designers. But because the wedding reception was to last from day into night, we realized that the crisp lines accentuated by daylight would be lost in the evening unless we paid extra attention to lighting. We decided to fill the room with candlelight and crystal, set on white linen. The glow of the candles was refracted through the crystal, filling the space with rainbows and sparkling light. This warm magic created the perfect atmosphere in which to celebrate a new union.

A loft offers endless possibilities.

Dilled Scallop Terrine
with Cucumber Leek Sauce

1 POUND SEA
    SCALLOPS
1 LARGE EGG WHITE
SALT AND PEPPER
    TO TASTE
1¼ CUPS HEAVY
    CREAM
1 TABLESPOON
    MINCED FRESH
    DILL
1 TABLESPOON
    MINCED FRESH
    CHIVES
1 LARGE CUCUMBER
6 TRIMMED DILL
    SPRIGS
CUCUMBER LEEK
    SAUCE

SERVES 12

Preheat the oven to 350°.

Cut half of the scallops into ½-inch dice. Set aside.

In a food processor, using the metal blade, purée the remaining scallops with the egg white. Add salt and pepper and slowly add the heavy cream with the motor running. Process until thick. Add the dill and chives and process just to blend.

Peel and seed the cucumber. Cut it into ⅜-inch strips. Place them in rapidly boiling salted water for 3 minutes, or until just cooked. Immediately remove them to ice water. When they are chilled, drain them and pat dry.

Generously butter a 1-quart terrine. Line it with parchment paper (baking paper) cut to fit exactly. Lay the dill sprigs in a decorative pattern across the bottom and pack a thin layer of purée on top to coat the bottom of the terrine.

Lay half the cucumber strips and half the diced scallops on top of the purée. Add a layer of purée and another layer of cucumbers and scallops, and cover with a final layer of purée.

Place the terrine in a water bath and bake for 1 hour, or until set. Cool on a wire rack for 30 minutes, then refrigerate for 3 hours.

When ready to serve, coat the bottom of each serving plate with Cucumber Leek Sauce. Unmold the terrine and slice it into pieces no more than ½-inch thick. Place 1 slice in the center of each plate and serve immediately

CUCUMBER LEEK SAUCE

1 BUNCH LEEKS,
    WHITE PARTS ONLY
1 LARGE CUCUMBER,
    10 INCHES LONG
1 TABLESPOON
    MINCED FRESH
    DILL
3 CUPS SOUR CREAM
SALT AND PEPPER
    TO TASTE

Wash the leeks thoroughly and drain until dry. Cut them cross-wise into very thin slices.

Peel and cut the cucumber in half lengthwise. Seed and slice it into paper-thin half moons, preferably on a mandolin.

Toss the vegetables with the dill, sour cream, salt and pepper. Cover and refrigerate for at least 1 hour.

Arrange the sliced duck breast in a fan shape.

BREAST OF DUCK
WITH CHARTREUSE

Remove the skin from the duck breasts and set it aside. Trim the breasts well and cut each in half. Rub each breast with the oil and toss them with crushed juniper berries, ground pepper, lemon rind, salt, and 1 tablespoon of the Chartreuse. Cover and refrigerate for 30 minutes.

Combine the softened butter with the remaining Chartreuse and set aside.

In a medium sauté pan over low heat, sauté the duck skin to render the fat. Pour off all but 1 tablespoon of the duck fat and discard the skins. Raise the heat to medium-high and sauté the chilled duck breasts in the fat for about 3 minutes per side, or until the outsides are well browned and the insides remain rare. Remove them from the pan and keep them warm.

Lower the heat and deglaze the sauté pan with the Chartreuse, butter, and the orange juice. When well combined, add the cream and cook for 5 minutes, or until reduced by one third. Add more salt and pepper if necessary.

Slice the warm breasts on the diagonal, keeping their shape. Fan the slices out slightly on a serving plate and coat them with the Chartreuse sauce. Serve immediately.

6 WHOLE DUCK
  BREASTS
2 TABLESPOONS
  CORN OIL
1 TABLESPOON
  FINELY CRUSHED
  JUNIPER BERRIES
1 TEASPOON FINELY
  GROUND PEPPER
1 TABLESPOON
  GRATED FRESH
  LEMON RIND
SALT TO TASTE
3 TABLESPOONS
  CHARTREUSE
½ CUP UNSALTED
  BUTTER,
  SOFTENED
½ CUP FRESH
  ORANGE JUICE
1½ CUPS HEAVY
  CREAM

SERVES 12

A setting in which no two tabletops are alike.

ZUCCHINI AND POTATOES ANNA

3½ POUNDS BAKING
    POTATOES
5 MEDIUM ZUCCHINI
1 CUP CLARIFIED
    BUTTER
SALT AND PEPPER
    TO TASTE

SERVES 12

Preheat the oven to 450°.

Peel and slice the potatoes ⅛-inch thick. Cover them with cold water and set aside.

Trim and cut the zucchini into ¼-inch slices. Lay them out on a paper towel and lay another towel on top to absorb the moisture.

Pour enough clarified butter into a large cast-iron skillet to fill it ¼-inch deep. Place the skillet over low heat.

Remove the potato slices from the water and dry them thoroughly. Arrange some of the slices in a circle, overlapping them, around the edge of the pan. Going in the opposite direction, arrange a circle of overlapping zucchini slices, slightly covering the inside edge of the potato circle.

Continue making alternating circles, adding the salt and pepper, until the pan is filled and the slices form a dome. Gently shake the pan from time to time to keep the vegetables from sticking.

Generously butter the bottom of a sauté pan that will fit inside the cast-iron skillet. Press it hard on top of the vegetables, forcing the layers together. Cover the skillet with aluminum foil and place it in the oven for 20 minutes. Uncover it and, again using the buttered sauté pan, press down hard on the vegetables. Return the skillet to the oven, uncovered, and bake for 25 minutes, or until the top layer of vegetables is crisp.

Remove the skillet from the oven and pour off any excess butter. Run a spatula around the edge of the skillet and invert it onto a serving platter. Serve immediately.

An all-white background lets the guests shine.

SAUTEED WATERCRESS AND RED RADISHES

6 BUNCHES
WATERCRESS
¼ CUP UNSALTED
BUTTER
1 TEASPOON MINCED
GARLIC

Trim 1 to 2 inches off the watercress, removing the thick stems but leaving some of the stalk.

Melt the butter in a large sauté pan over low heat. Add the garlic and sauté for 2 minutes, or until the garlic is soft.

Immediately add the watercress and radishes. Raise the heat and sauté for 2 minutes, or until the vegetables are just warm but still crisp. Add salt and pepper and serve immediately.

3 CUPS THINLY
SLICED RED
RADISHES
SALT AND PEPPER
TO TASTE

SERVES 12

CHOCOLATE DIPPED STRAWBERRIES

Wash and dry the strawberries, being careful not to bruise them.

Melt the chocolate in the top half of a double boiler over boiling water. Reduce the heat and keep the chocolate warm.

Holding a strawberry by the stem, gently dip it into the melted chocolate to coat approximately three quarters of the berry. Lay it out on waxed paper to set. Refrigerate the dipped berries until ready to serve.

24 LARGE, LONG-
STEMMED
STRAWBERRIES
½ POUND GLAZING
OR DIPPING
CHOCOLATE

SERVES 12

The Phantom of the Opera Supper

OYSTERS BIENVILLE

PHEASANT PIE

SALADE FRISEE WITH FENNEL AND RADISH

CHESTNUT CHARLOTTE WITH CREME ANGLAISE

Transforming a neglected landmark theater in New York City into the scene of a smash hit opening-night party was no small accomplishment. Through a careful manipulation of space, lighting, and sound, it rivaled the Paris Opera House.

First, a platform was constructed on top of the orchestra seats, raising the main floor level with the stage. When the guests arrived, they made their grand entrance right "on stage." The tables were set in Belle Epoque style; music from *The Phantom of the Opera* echoed throughout the hall; and images from the original film were projected against the back wall. As more and more guests gathered, creaking noises began to reverberate throughout the theater. Suddenly, a section of the floor opened. From deep within the orchestra pit, a grand-scale Wurlitzer organ emerged, with the Phantom himself at the keyboard. Even the most sophisticated theatergoer was enthralled with his performance.

Sharing the stage with your guests.

OYSTERS BIENVILLE

3 TABLESPOONS
UNSALTED
BUTTER

½ CUP MINCED
SCALLIONS, WHITE
PART ONLY

¼ CUP ALL-PURPOSE
FLOUR

1 CUP CLAM BROTH

1 POUND SHRIMP,
COOKED,
CLEANED,
DEVEINED, AND
MINCED

1⅓ CUPS MINCED
BUTTON
MUSHROOMS

3 LARGE EGG YOLKS

⅓ CUP DRY WHITE
WINE

¾ CUP HEAVY CREAM

SALT AND PEPPER
TO TASTE

TABASCO SAUCE TO
TASTE

36 BLUE POINT
OYSTERS,
CLEANED AND
OPENED ON THE
HALF SHELL

1 TABLESPOON
HUNGARIAN
PAPRIKA

SERVES 12

Preheat the oven to 400°.

Melt the butter in a medium saucepan over low heat. Add the scallions and sauté for about 3 minutes, or until soft.

Stir in the flour and whisk to combine. Add the clam broth. Raise the heat, whisking constantly, to blend in the clam broth.

Stir in the shrimp and mushrooms.

Whisk together the egg yolks, wine, and cream and quickly stir this into the shrimp mixture. Add salt and pepper and Tabasco sauce to taste and cook for 3 minutes, stirring constantly, until thick.

Spoon the sauce over the oysters to cover. Sprinkle them with the paprika. Place them on a baking sheet and bake for 3 minutes, or until bubbling. Serve immediately.

PHEASANT PIE

4 YOUNG
PHEASANTS,
DRESSED

12 JUNIPER BERRIES

2 BAY LEAVES

1 SPRING FRESH
ROSEMARY

SALT AND PEPPER
TO TASTE

½ CUP UNSALTED
BUTTER

½ CUP WHITE WINE

¼ CUP COGNAC

½ CUP MINCED
FRESH SHALLOTS

¾ CUP CHOPPED
CELERY

18 GOLDEN OAK
MUSHROOMS (OR
ANY OTHER FRESH
MUSHROOM), SLICED

18 BABY CARROTS,
PEELED AND
BLANCHED

2 CUPS PEELED AND
DICED POTATOES

TART DOUGH (SEE
PAGE 29)

SERVES 12

Using a boning knife, remove the skin from the pheasants and discard it. Slice off the breast and leg meat and set it aside.

Place the pheasant carcasses, juniper berries, bay leaves, rosemary, and salt and pepper in a stock pot. Cover with cold water and bring to a boil over high heat. Lower the heat and simmer for 2 hours. Strain the stock through a fine sieve into a saucepan. (Discard the spices and berries.) Return the stock to the heat and continue cooking until it is reduced to 3 cups.

Slice the pheasant breast and leg meat into thin strips. Melt ¼ cup of the butter in a heavy sauté pan over medium heat. Add the pheasant meat and sauté for 2 minutes, or until the meat just begins to brown. Remove the pheasant from the heat and keep it warm.

Pour the white wine and cognac into the sauté pan. Raise the heat and cook for about 5 minutes, or until the mixture is reduced by two thirds. Add the stock and continue cooking for about 20 minutes, or until the liquid is syrupy. Immediately begin to incorporate 2 tablespoons of the remaining butter, a bit at a time.

In another sauté pan, melt the last 2 tablespoons of butter over low heat. Add the shallots, celery, and mushrooms and sauté for 4 minutes. Remove from the heat and whisk this mixture into the sauce.

Combine the sauce and meat, and pour into a deep casserole. Add the carrots and potatoes.

Preheat the oven to 400°.

Roll out the tart dough to ⅛-inch thick and cut it into a circle to fit the top of the casserole. Crimp the edges to seal, and prick the top with a fork.

Bake for 30 minutes, or until golden. Let rest for 5 minutes before serving.

Oysters Bienville.

Pheasant Pie.

SALADE FRISEE WITH FENNEL AND RADISH

3 BUNCHES FRISEE
(OR CHICORY)

6 OUNCES GRUYERE
CHEESE

2½ CUPS SLICED
FRESH FENNEL

1 CUP EXTRA VIRGIN
OLIVE OIL

1 LARGE LEMON

SALT AND PEPPER
TO TASTE

3 CUPS SLICED RED
RADISHES

½ CUP CHOPPED
FRESH ITALIAN
PARSLEY

SERVES 12

Wash, trim and separate the frisée. Dry it thoroughly.

Using a cheese slicer, cut the Gruyère into very thin slices. Cover and set it aside.

Place equal portions of the frisée on 12 salad plates. Top them with equal portions of sliced fennel. Drizzle with one third of the oil and a squeeze of juice from the lemon, and add salt and pepper. Cover the fennel with a layer of sliced radishes and season again as above.

Top the radishes with equal portions of cheese slices and chopped parsley. Season the salad with the remaining olive oil, lemon juice, and salt and pepper. Serve immediately.

CHESTNUT CHARLOTTE WITH CREME ANGLAISE

8 TEASPOONS
UNFLAVORED
GELATIN

4 TABLESPOONS
RUM

4 CUPS MILK

12 LARGE EGG
YOLKS

1⅓ CUPS SUGAR

1 CUP CHESTNUT
PUREE

¼ CUP CHESTNUT
SYRUP

1 TEASPOON
VANILLA EXTRACT

4 CUPS HEAVY
CREAM, WHIPPED

1 CUP CHOPPED
MARRONS GLACEE

LADYFINGERS

CREME ANGLAISE

SERVES 12

Mix the gelatin and rum together and set aside.

In a heavy saucepan, over medium heat, scald the milk. Let it cool slightly.

Beat the egg yolks, gradually beating in the sugar until thick and pale yellow. Slowly pour the warm milk into the eggs. Pour into a heavy saucepan and cook, stirring constantly, over medium heat for about 10 minutes or until the mixture coats a spoon. Whisk in the gelatin and rum and stir to blend.

Slowly whisk the custard into the chestnut purée. Add the chestnut syrup and vanilla, and stir to blend.

Place in the freezer for about 30 minutes, stirring frequently, until the mixture is cool. When cool, fold in the whipped cream and chopped marron glacée.

Butter the sides of two 7½-inch Charlotte molds. Cut a parchment paper (baking paper) circle to fit the bottom of each mold and line the sides with the Ladyfingers. Pour an equal amount of the chestnut mixture into each mold. Cover with a piece of waxed paper and refrigerate for at least 2 hours before serving. (If desired, you may decorate the top with whipped cream rosettes and pieces of marron glacée.)

To serve, coat the bottom of a service plate with Crème Anglaise and place a slice of the Charlotte in the center.

LADYFINGERS

Preheat the oven to 350°.

Stir ¼ cup of the sugar into the egg yolks. In the bowl of an electric mixer, beat the egg yolks until thick and pale yellow. Add the vanilla and stir to combine.

Beat the egg whites until they hold a peak, gradually adding the remaining sugar. Gently fold in the cornstarch, followed by the egg yolks. Finally, very gently, fold in the flour.

Using a pastry tube fitted with a ⅜-inch in diameter round plain tip, pipe the batter, in 4-inch long sections, onto a parchment-lined baking sheet. Dust with confectioners' sugar and bake for 8 minutes, or until light gold.

Remove from the oven. When slightly cooled, remove from the baking sheet and finish cooling on wire racks.

12 LARGE EGG YOLKS
1 CUP PLUS 2 TABLESPOONS SUGAR
1 TEASPOON VANILLA EXTRACT
8 LARGE EGG WHITES
1 CUP CORNSTARCH
1 ¼ CUPS FLOUR
CONFECTIONERS' SUGAR

MAKES ABOUT 24

CREME ANGLAISE

Scald the milk in a heavy saucepan over medium heat. Split and scrape the inside of the vanilla bean, placing its contents in the pan with milk. Add the lemon rind. Whisk in the sugar. Pour half of the scalded milk into the egg yolks, then pour this mixture back into the remaining milk. Bring to a boil, stirring constantly. Reduce the heat and continue stirring constantly, for 1 minute. Strain and cool.

3 CUPS MILK
1 2-INCH PIECE VANILLA BEAN
GRATED RIND OF 1 LEMON
¾ CUP SUGAR
6 LARGE EGG YOLKS, BEATEN

Chestnut Charlotte with Crème Anglaise.

A Summer Wedding

TRIO OF SEAFOOD PACKETS
WITH SAFFRON SAUCE

MEDALLIONS OF VEAL WITH CITRUS,
CHAMPAGNE, AND CAVIAR

ASPARAGUS TIPS

SPECIALTY WEDDING CAKE

TRUFFLES

Roses and summer, tents and weddings, sailboats and shimmering water—perfect combinations for happiness. With this reception's romantic waterside setting, a tent created the essential intimate space. Guests could mingle outside or circulate under the shade offered by the tent, while the harbor's panorama of sailboats presented an everchanging yet serene backdrop. As dusk approached, small lights ensconced in chiffon and ribbons twinkled, starlike on the ceiling of the tent. Garden-fresh blush roses on each table added that personal touch that made the guests feel welcome, and very much a part of the family celebration.

The softness of a summer breeze captured on a tabletop.

A Trio of Seafood Packets makes an elegant first course.

TRIO OF SEAFOOD PACKETS
WITH SAFFRON SAUCE

1 POUND PLUS 3
   WHOLE SEA
   SCALLOPS
¼ CUP DRY
   VERMOUTH
2 LARGE EGGS
2 LARGE EGG WHITES
¾ CUP HEAVY CREAM
SALT AND WHITE
   PEPPER TO TASTE
4 LARGE LEEKS
12 LARGE NAPA
   CABBAGE LEAVES
12 LARGE SPINACH
   LEAVES

Preheat the oven to 350°.

Blend 1 pound of the scallops and vermouth in a food processor using the metal blade. Add the eggs and egg whites and blend for 1 minute. Remove from the processor bowl and push through a fine sieve into a bowl, which has been packed in chopped ice. Using a wooden spoon, gradually blend in the cream. Add salt and pepper. Pour into a buttered 1-quart square baking dish and cover with aluminum foil. Place the dish into a larger pan. Pour enough of the water into the larger pan to come halfway up the filled pan.

Place in the oven and bake for 15 minutes or until the scallop mousse is firm. Remove the scallop mousse from the oven and pan of water. Cool on a wire rack.

Trim the leeks of most of the green and cut them in half, lengthwise. Wash thoroughly and pat dry. Select 24 large unblemished outer leaves. Wash the cabbage and spinach leaves and pat them dry.

6 CUPS WATER
½ TEASPOON COARSE
   SALT
2 TEASPOONS
   UNSALTED
   BUTTER
6 SHELLED RAW
   OYSTERS
⅓ POUND COOKED
   LOBSTER MEAT
SAFFRON SAUCE
¼ CUP CHOPPED
   FRESH CHIVES

SERVES 12

Fabric and flowers soften hard edges.

Bring the water and coarse salt to a boil over high heat. Add the vegetables, one kind at a time, and quickly blanch until just slightly pliable. As each kind of leaf is blanched, remove it from the water with a slotted spoon and immediately immerse it in iced water. When cool, remove the leaves from the iced water and drain them on paper towels. Pat the leaves dry.

Cut the remaining scallops into quarters. Cut the oysters in half, then place the scallops and oysters on a paper towel to drain dry, always keeping the oysters and scallops separate.

Melt the butter in a small sauté pan over low heat. When warm, add the scallops and oysters, keeping them separate, and sauté for 1 minute or until slightly firm. Remove them from the heat and drain well.

Remove the central rib from the blanched cabbage and spinach leaves, being careful not to tear the leaves. Lay each leaf out flat on waxed paper.

To make the seafood packets, first place equal portions of the lobster meat into the center of each cabbage leaf. Add 1 tablespoon of scallop mousse. Then fold the leaf into a tight square packet. Continue until you have made 12 packets.

Next place 1 piece of the sautéed scallop and 1 tablespoon of the scallop mousse into each spinach leaf. Fold the leaf into a tight square packet, and make 12 packets.

Crisscross the leeks. Place half of an oyster and 1 tablespoon of the scallop mousse into the center. Fold the leeks over to form a tight square packet. If necessary, trim off any excess. Again make 12 packets.

Place each packet onto the rack of a steamer and steam for 8 minutes over boiling water. Remove from the steamer. Keep warm.

Pour equal portions of the Saffron Sauce over the bottom of each of the 12 serving plates. Place 1 trio of vegetable packets in the center of each plate. Garnish with chopped chives and serve immediately.

SAFFRON SAUCE

1 TEASPOON SAFFRON
1 CUP PLUS 1 TABLESPOON DRY WHITE WINE
2 CUPS FISH STOCK (SEE PAGE 126)
¼ CUP CHOPPED SHALLOTS
2 CLOVES GARLIC, MINCED
PINCH HERBES DE PROVENCE
1 TEASPOON GRATED FRESH GINGER ROOT
2 CUPS HEAVY CREAM
4 TABLESPOONS SALTED BUTTER
¼ CUP FRESH LEMON JUICE
SALT AND WHITE PEPPER TO TASTE

Crumble the saffron threads into 1 tablespoon of wine and set it aside to soak.

Place the Fish Stock in a medium sauce pan over high heat. Bring it to a boil and add the shallots, garlic, Herbes de Provence, ginger root, and 1 cup of wine. Lower the heat and simmer until the liquid is reduced by two thirds. When reduced, remove the stock from the heat and strain it through a fine sieve into a small saucepan.

Place the saucepan over medium heat and bring the stock to a simmer. Whisk in the cream and wine-soaked saffron. Simmer, stirring frequently, for 5 minutes. Then, whisk in the butter, 1 teaspoon at a time. When well combined, whisk in the lemon juice and salt and pepper. Serve immediately.

MEDALLIONS OF VEAL WITH CITRUS, CHAMPAGNE, AND CAVIAR

24 2½-OUNCE VEAL
  LOIN FILLETS,
  ABOUT ½-INCH
  THICK
¼ CUP FINELY
  JULIENNED FRESH
  LIME PEEL
¼ CUP FINELY
  JULIENNED FRESH
  ORANGE PEEL
24 LIME SECTIONS
  (ABOUT 3–4 LIMES)
36 ORANGE
  SECTIONS (ABOUT
  8–10 ORANGES)
¼ CUP SALTED
  BUTTER
1 TABLESPOON
  MINCED SHALLOTS
½ TEASPOON MINCED
  FRESH GARLIC
2 TABLESPOONS
  WHITE WINE
  VINEGAR
1 CUP CHAMPAGNE
4 CUPS VEAL STOCK
  (SEE PAGE 133)

Gently pound the veal with the side of a cleaver (or any flattening tool) to slightly flatten. Season with salt and pepper, and dust with flour. Set the veal aside.

Place the julienned lime and orange in rapidly boiling water for 30 seconds. Drain and place in iced water. When cool, drain and pat dry. Set aside.

Keeping the fruits separate, peel the membrane from the orange and lime sections, being careful to keep the sections whole. Set them aside.

Melt 2 tablespoons of butter in a medium saucepan over low heat. Add the shallots and garlic, and sauté for 5 minutes or until soft. Add the vinegar. Raise the heat to medium and stir to deglaze the pan. Add the champagne, Veal Stock, herbs, salt, and white pepper. Lower the heat and simmer, stirring constantly, until it has reduced by half.

In a separate saucepan, reduce the cream by half over medium heat. Strain the reduced stock into the reduced cream, whisking constantly.

Blend the orange juice and arrowroot, and whisk into the cream. Lower the heat and simmer for 2 minutes. Remove from the heat and whisk in 2 tablespoons of the butter, a bit at a time. Whisk until it is well incorporated. Keep warm over warm water until ready to serve.

Combine the clarified butter and olive oil. Heat about 2 table-spoons of the combined butter and oil at a time in a large sauté pan over high heat. When hot, add the veal medallions, a few at a time, and sear on each side for 30 seconds. Wipe the pan clean from time to time to keep the butter from burning. Keep the veal warm as you sear all the medallions.

Gently fold the caviar into the warm champagne sauce. Ladle equal portions of the sauce onto 12 warm serving plates. Place 2 medallions on each plate. Sprinkle with the citrus julienne and garnish the side of each portion with 3 orange sections and 2 lime sections. Serve immediately.

½ TEASPOON DRIED
  THYME
2 MEDIUM BAY
  LEAVES
¼ TEASPOON
  GROUND NUTMEG
SALT AND WHITE
  PEPPER TO TASTE
2 CUPS HEAVY
  CREAM
⅓ CUP FRESH
  ORANGE JUICE
1 ½ TEASPOONS
  ARROWROOT
½ CUP CLARIFIED
  BUTTER
1 CUP ALL-PURPOSE
  FLOUR
¼ CUP OLIVE OIL
2 OUNCES AMERICAN
  STURGEON CAVIAR

SERVES 12

The richness of the champagne and caviar sauce is balanced by the refreshing tartness of citrus.

ASPARAGUS TIPS

Trim the tough ends from the asparagus. Using a vegetable peeler, peel away the rough outer skin around the trimmed ends.

Place the stalks in an asparagus poacher or a vegetable steamer over rapidly boiling water. Steam for about 3 minutes or until tender.

Remove from the heat and gently toss in the clarified butter, adding salt and pepper. Serve immediately.

60 SLIM STALKS FRESH ASPARAGUS
¼ CUP CLARIFIED BUTTER
SALT AND WHITE PEPPER TO TASTE

SERVES 12

The magnificent wedding cake.

CHOCOLATE TRUFFLES

Melt the chocolate in the top half of a double boiler over rapidly boiling water. Keep warm.

Place the cream and sugar in a small saucepan over medium heat. Whisk constantly until the sugar is dissolved. Then whisk in the chocolate and cognac until well blended. Remove from the heat.

When the chocolate has cooled and thickened, form into bite-size balls. Place the balls on a baking sheet and refrigerate for at least 1 hour, or until quite firm.

Just before serving, roll the chocolate balls in cocoa powder. Shake off any excess and serve immediately.

8 OUNCES SEMI-SWEET CHOCOLATE
¾ CUP HEAVY CREAM
¼ CUP SUGAR
2 TABLESPOONS COGNAC
¼ CUP SIFTED COCOA POWDER

SERVES 12

Onstage at Carnegie Hall

ASSORTED AMUSE GUEULES

SEAFOOD BOUDINS WITH TOMATO SEMIFREDDO

FILET MIGNON WITH WATERCRESS
AND WALNUTS

ROESTI POTATOES

SAUTEED BABY VEGETABLES

LES FRIANDISES

At the triumphant conclusion of a capital campaign fund for the restoration of Carnegie Hall, major donors, and corporate and civic leaders gathered to toast the accomplishment. After ceremonies, a private concert was held in the refurbished Carnegie Hall. With the final "Bravo," guests were led to tables on stage, where they dined facing the awe-inspiring renovated hall. This celebration of gracious social responsibility paved the way for expanding the growing family of those who support the vital institution.

The ultimate measure of achievement—Carnegie Hall.

ASSORTED AMUSE GUEULES

TART DOUGH (SEE PAGE 29)

PUFF PASTRY (SEE PAGE 151)

ANCHOVY PASTE

SMOKED FISH

SMOKED MEATS

WILD MUSHROOMS

CHEESES (PREFERABLY CREAMY)

AVOCADO

Amuse gueules—French for "to entertain the mouth"—are bite-sized palate-teasers, flavorful hors d'oeuvres made of simple savory fillings wrapped in tart dough or puff pastry, and shaped into rounds, pinwheels, or whatever you fancy. Some easy fillings are anchovy paste, smoked fish or smoked meats, wild mushroom duxelle (consisting of chopped mushrooms sautéed in butter), cheeses, and avocado. Whatever you choose, each completed *amuse gueule* should be no more than a ½ wide. Allow at least 6 pieces per person.

A flower arrangement that does not interfere with sight lines.

SEAFOOD BOUDINS WITH TOMATO SEMIFREDDO

½ POUND SHRIMP, PEELED AND DEVEINED

1 POUND FILLET OF LEMON SOLE

4 LARGE EGG WHITES

1 ½ TEASPOONS MINCED FRESH SHALLOTS

2 TEASPOONS MINCED FRESH CHIVES

1 TABLESPOON MINCED FRESH PARSLEY

2 ½ TEASPOONS DRY VERMOUTH

PINCH CAYENNE PEPPER

PINCH GROUND NUTMEG

SALT AND PEPPER TO TASTE

2 CUPS HEAVY CREAM

½ POUND MINCED FRESH BAY SCALLOPS

8 CUPS FRESH FISH STOCK (SEE PAGE 126)

TOMATO SEMIFREDDO

1 CUP CHOPPED FRESH ITALIAN PARSLEY

SERVES 12

In a food processor, using the metal blade, purée the shrimp and sole until smooth. Add the egg whites, one at a time, with the motor running. Process for 5 seconds.

Add the shallots, chives, parsley, vermouth, cayenne, nutmeg, and salt and pepper to taste. When blended, keep the motor running and pour in the cream in a slow steady stream.

Remove the mixture from the processor bowl and stir in the scallops. Cover and refrigerate for 1 hour.

Remove the seafood from the refrigerator and divide it into 12 equal portions. Lay each portion on a double layer of clear plastic food wrap, leaving 1½-inch of plastic on each end. Enfold the seafood and roll the plastic tightly into a sausage shape. Firmly tie each end with kitchen twine.

Bring the Fish Stock to a boil in a stock pot over high heat. Add the seafood sausages. Lower the heat and simmer for 15 minutes, or until done. Remove the sausages from the stock and cool them on a wire rack.

Untie and unwrap the sausages. Pour some of the Tomato Semifreddo onto the bottom of each of 12 plates. Lay a seafood boudin in the center and sprinkle with the chopped parsley. Serve immediately.

Seafood Boudins with Tomato Semifreddo.

TOMATO SEMIFREDDO

2½ POUNDS PLUM
    TOMATOES
1½ TABLESPOONS
    OLIVE OIL
1 TABLESPOON
    MINCED FRESH
    GARLIC

SALT AND PEPPER
    TO TASTE
1 TEASPOON SUGAR
2 TABLESPOONS
    CHOPPED ITALIAN
    PARSLEY

Peel, seed, and chop the tomatoes.

Heat the olive oil in a medium sauté pan over low heat. Add the garlic and sauté for 3 minutes. Stir in the tomatoes and salt and pepper to taste. Raise the heat and simmer for 5 minutes. Add the sugar and chopped parsley and cook for an additional 3 minutes.

Remove the sauce from the heat and serve it hot or at room temperature.

FILET MIGNON WITH WATERCRESS AND WALNUTS

1 7-POUND FILET MIGNON

6 BUNCHES WATERCRESS

3 TABLESPOONS SALTED BUTTER

¾ CUP CHOPPED ONION

1 CUP CHOPPED FRESH SHALLOTS

1 TABLESPOON CHOPPED GARLIC

¾ CUP CHOPPED WALNUTS

2 TABLESPOONS OLIVE OIL

SALT AND PEPPER TO TASTE

CREAMY MUSTARD SAUCE

SERVES 12

Preheat the oven to 500°.

Make a hole through the center of the trimmed filet mignon with the handle of a wooden spoon. Set it aside.

Trim the watercress of all large stems and poach it for 30 seconds in rapidly boiling water. Immediately remove and place it in ice water. When chilled, drain and squeeze it dry. Set aside.

Heat the butter in a medium sauté pan over low heat. Add the onion, shallots, and garlic, and sauté for 4 minutes, or until they are soft.

Combine the watercress, walnuts, and sautéed vegetables. When they are well blended, stuff them into the cavity of the filet mignon.

Tie the filet up so that it keeps its shape while roasting. Rub it with olive oil, salt and pepper, and place on a roasting pan. Roast for 12 minutes; then turn and roast the other side for 12 more minutes.

Remove the filet from the oven and let it set for 10 minutes before carving. Serve with the Creamy Mustard Sauce.

CREAMY MUSTARD SAUCE

½ CUP UNSALTED BUTTER

2 TABLESPOONS MINCED FRESH SHALLOTS

⅓ CUP DRY WHITE WINE

⅛ CUP POMMERY MUSTARD

Heat the butter in a small sauté pan over low heat. Add the shallots and sauté for 3 minutes, or until they are wilted. Add the wine. Cook for 10 minutes, or until it has reduced by half.

When the sauce has reduced, stir in the mustards, cream, sugar, and pepper. Cook, over low heat, stirring frequently, for 10 minutes or until thick.

⅓ CUP DIJON MUSTARD

1 CUP HEAVY CREAM

1 TEASPOON SUGAR

⅛ TEASPOON PEPPER

The entrée ready to be served.

Roesti Potatoes

Peel the potatoes. Using a melon baller, cut the potatoes into balls. Each pound should yield approximately 15 potato balls.

Melt the butter in a large sauté pan over medium heat. Add the potatoes, and salt and pepper. Sauté, stirring frequently, for 15 minutes, or until the potatoes are cooked through and are golden brown. Serve hot.

4 POUNDS IDAHO POTATOES
½ CUP SALTED BUTTER
SALT AND WHITE PEPPER TO TASTE

SERVES 12

Sauteed Baby Vegetables

Peel the carrots, leaving a trace of the stem. Wash and trim the zucchini and the yellow and patty pan squashes.

Place the carrots into rapidly boiling salted water for 2 minutes, or until just slightly cooked and still crisp. Immediately place them in ice water. When chilled, drain and pat them dry.

Melt the butter in a large sauté pan over medium heat. Add the vegetables, salt and pepper to taste, and sauté for 3 minutes, or until the vegetables are heated through and just slightly cooked.

Serve immediately.

12 BABY CARROTS
16 BABY ZUCCHINI
16 BABY YELLOW SQUASH
16 BABY PATTY PAN SQUASH
¼ CUP SALTED BUTTER
SALT AND PEPPER TO TASTE

SERVES 12

Les Friandises

Les friandises are simply appetizing arrangements of dainty sweets. Petit fours, tiny molded cookies, or marzipan and beautiful chocolates are some suggestions available from fine bakeries. Perfect miniature fruits and berries and edible flowers, such as pansies and nasturtiums, can add interest and variety.

Les Friandises.

Una Serenata Gastronomica

TUNA CARPACCIO WITH BOTTARGO

RICOTTA RAVIOLI WITH FENNEL
AND PIGNOLI BUTTER

QUAIL WITH BLOOD ORANGES

CHOCOLATE HAZELNUT TORTA

Truly magical moments occur when all the elements of an event are perfectly balanced. Such was the case at the Serenata Gastronomica.

A Baroque ballroom set the stage for the introduction of some special Sicilian wines. Our challenge was to marry the mood, the music, and the menu to the subtle qualities of these vintages. The evening followed a sonata format—beginning with palate teasers, the lightest white, and the gentlest sounds and building to a crescendo that featured the most prized new red. The coda for this serenata came when the host and guests goined the musicians in singing a classic Italian lullaby.

The serenata overture.

TOP *Tuna Carpaccio with Bottargo.* ABOVE *Ricotta Ravioli with Fennel and Pignoli Butter.*

TUNA CARPACCIO WITH BOTTARGO

12 3-OUNCE SLICES
   FRESH TUNA
2¼ CUPS OLIVE OIL
¾ CUP FRESH LEMON
   JUICE
1 TEASPOON
   GROUND PEPPER

Place the tuna between sheets of oiled, waxed, or parchment paper (baking paper), and pound them to flatten slightly.

Place each piece of tuna on a salad plate.

Whisk the olive oil, lemon juice, and pepper until well combined, and drizzle over the tuna.

Grate the Bottargo over each slice of tuna and sprinkle it with chopped parsley.

3 OUNCES
   BOTTARGO
   CHEESE*
½ CUP CHOPPED
   ITALIAN PARSLEY

SERVES 12

NOTE: INGREDIENTS
   MARKED WITH AN AS-
   TERISK (*) ARE AVAIL-
   ABLE FROM ITALIAN
   SPECIALTY STORES.

RICOTTA RAVIOLI WITH FENNEL AND PIGNOLI BUTTER

Combine the flour, 4 of the eggs, the olive oil, and salt in the bowl of a food processor. Using the metal blade, process for about 3 minutes, or until a smooth dough is formed.

Roll the dough out on a lightly floured board to about 1/16-inch thick. Cut it into 48 3-inch circles. Cover and let rest.

In an electric mixer, beat the ricotta, remaining eggs, parsley, 3 tablespoons of the Parmesan cheese, and salt and pepper to taste until well combined.

Place a heaping tablespoon of ricotta mixture in the center of each of 24 dough circles. Place another circle on top and press the edges together with a fork, making certain that they are sealed.

Cook the ravioli in gently boiling salted water for 5 minutes. Drain well.

Place 2 ravioli on each serving plate. Spoon the Fennel and Pignoli Butter on top. Sprinkle with the remaining Parmesan cheese and chopped tomatoes. Serve immediately.

4 CUPS ALL-
   PURPOSE FLOUR
7 LARGE EGGS
¼ CUP OLIVE OIL
SALT TO TASTE
3½ CUPS RICOTTA
   CHEESE
3 TABLESPOONS
   MINCED FRESH
   ITALIAN PARSLEY
1 CUP GRATED
   PARMESAN
   CHEESE
WHITE PEPPER TO
   TASTE
FENNEL AND PIGNOLI
   BUTTER
2 CUPS CHOPPED
   AND SEEDED PLUM
   TOMATOES

SERVES 12

FENNEL AND PIGNOLI BUTTER

1 LARGE HEAD
   FRESH FENNEL
1 CUP UNSALTED
   BUTTER
1 TEASPOON MINCED
   FRESH SAGE

Wash and trim the fennel. Chop it very fine.

Heat the butter in a large sauté pan over low heat. Add the fennel and sage, and sauté for 3 minutes, until the fennel is soft. Stir in the pignoli nuts and salt and pepper.

¼ CUP TOASTED
   PIGNOLI NUTS
SALT AND PEPPER
   TO TASTE

QUAIL WITH BLOOD ORANGES

2 CUPS UNSALTED BUTTER

½ CUP DICED RED ONION

¼ CUP DICED CELERY

½ CUP MARSALA WINE

1 LOAF CRUSTY, DENSE ITALIAN BREAD, CUBED

1 TEASPOON MINCED FRESH MINT

3 CUPS FRESH POMEGRANATE SEEDS

SALT AND PEPPER TO TASTE

24 QUAIL, CLEANED, WASHED, AND DRAINED

¼ POUND PANCETTA, DICED (OR OTHER VERY LEAN BACON)*

1 TABLESPOON CHOPPED SAGE LEAVES

6–8 BLOOD ORANGES, PEELED AND SLICED

SERVES 12

Melt 1 cup of the butter in a large sauté pan over low heat. Add the onion and celery. Raise the heat to medium and sauté for 5 minutes, or until they are soft.

Pour ¼ cup of the Marsala into the pan and stir to deglaze. Add the bread cubes, mint, 2 cups of the pomegranate seeds, and salt and pepper. Stir to blend.

Remove the pan from the heat and let it cool.

Stuff each quail with the cooled stuffing.

Preheat the oven to 400°.

Melt ½ cup of the butter in a large sauté pan. Add the cubed pancetta and sauté for 7 minutes, or until the pancetta begins to brown.

Add the quail, a few at a time, and sauté for about 15 minutes, or until the quail is well browned and almost cooked through. Add more butter as necessary. When all the quail are browned, add the sage and the rest of the Marsala to the pan and deglaze. Add more of the butter to enrich the sauce, if necessary.

Place the quail on a baking sheet and spoon some of the pan juices over them. Roast for 5 minutes.

Place 2 of the quail on a bed of blood oranges on each serving plate. Spoon some of the pan juices over the top and sprinkle with the remaining pomegranate seeds.

Quail with Blood Oranges highlighted with pomegranate seeds.

CHOCOLATE HAZELNUT TORTA

8 OUNCES UNSWEETENED CHOCOLATE

1 CUP UNSALTED BUTTER

8 LARGE EGG YOLKS

1¼ CUPS GRANULATED SUGAR

5 LARGE EGG WHITES

1 CUP CHOPPED TOASTED HAZELNUTS

2 TABLESPOONS CONFECTIONERS' SUGAR

1 CUP HEAVY CREAM

½ TEASPOON INSTANT EXPRESSO COFFEE POWDER

SERVES 12

Preheat the oven to 350°.

Butter a 10-inch spring-form pan and set it aside.

Melt the chocolate and butter in the top half of a double boiler over hot water.

Beat the egg yolks and sugar with an electric mixer until thick and pale yellow. Stir the chocolate and butter into the egg yolks and whisk to blend.

Beat the egg whites until stiff. Fold them into the chocolate mixture until well blended.

Pour three quarters of the batter into the prepared pan. Bake for 25 minutes, or until set.

Remove the pan from the oven and cool it on a wire rack.

Remove the cake from the spring-form pan. Spread the remaining batter on top and cover it with hazelnuts. Dust it with confectioners' sugar.

Whip the cream and instant coffee powder into stiff peaks. Serve next to each slice of cake.

The perfect music at every party—lively conversation.

EVERY NATION HAS ITS OWN EXPRESSION TO DESCRIBE THAT WONDERFUL COMBINATION OF GRA-
cious hosting and joyful receiving—the pleasure of give and take between people. The Thai
spirit of *sanuk*, the Hawaiian *aloha*, the Italian *abbondanza*, the French *joie de vivre*—all
celebrate the individual in communion.

Enjoyment is sensing the moment, not defining it. Enjoyment is realizing that parties
need not necessarily be perfect but that they must be lively. When you have carefully
planned in advance, you can self-assuredly "dive in," savor the moment, and enjoy the most
important element of your creation—your guests.

We began this book with a party expressing the theme "The Best of the Best." That concept
sums up everything about hosts, parties, and guests. To be the best host, you will call upon
the very best of everything that brings enjoyment to your life and to your guests. That
enjoyment will breathe life into the creation of your party.

We hope that *New York Parties: The Art of Hosting* has started you on the road to discovering
the best of the best of yourself—your style.